# Polignac's Texas Brigade

# Polignac's Texas Brigade

## BY ALWYN BARR

*With a New Preface*

Texas A&M University Press
College Station, Texas

The paper used in this book meets the minimum requirements
of the American National Standard for Permanence
of Paper for Printed Library Materials, Z39.48-1984.
Binding materials have been chosen for durability.

Library of Congress Cataloging-in-Publication Data

Barr, Alwyn.
    Polignac's Texas Brigade / Alwyn Barr.
        p.    cm. — (Texas A&M University military history
series ; no. 60)
    Originally published: 1st ed. Houston : Texas Gulf
Coast Historical Association, 1964. With new pref.
    Includes bibliographical references and index.
    ISBN 0-89096-814-4
    1. Confederate States of America. Army. Texas
Cavalry. Polignac's Brigade. 2. United States—
History—Civil War, 1861–1865—Regimental histories.
3. Southwest, Old—History—Civil War, 1861–1865—
Regimental histories. 4. Texas—History—Civil War,
1861–1865—Regimental histories. I. Title. II. Series:
Texas A&M University military history series ; 60.
E580.4.P65B37    1998
973.7′464—dc21                                    97-51441
                                                          CIP

*For my mother and father,*
*Wilma Matlock Barr and Chester Alwyn Barr, Sr.*

# Contents

# Illustrations

# Preface to the 1998 Edition

Unit histories such as *Polignac's Texas Brigade* form a basic component of the extensive writings about the Civil War. Although the number of unit histories, both the early accounts of the conflict by former soldiers and more recent examinations of the struggle, has grown, these histories generally focus on companies and regiments. Studies of larger units, such as brigades and divisions, are far less common. When this volume first appeared, there had been full histories of only one Texas division, Walker's infantry, and three Texas brigades—Hood's infantry, Ross's cavalry, and Green's cavalry. All were written by men who had served in those units. Since then historians have added accounts of three Texas brigades: Hood's infantry, Parsons's cavalry, and Granbury's infantry.[1]

Beyond their value in clarifying the history of specific units, such studies also provide important insights into how the stages of battles fit together and unfolded. Furthermore, unit accounts offer the most detailed picture of the everyday lives of soldiers. As historians increasingly try to understand the impact of war on individuals and society, they also recognize that some aspects of the war beyond the battlefield undercut morale—clearly a problem at times for the men of Polignac's brigade. Historians in the late twentieth century continue to debate the impact of such factors on victory and defeat,

---

[1] C. E. Dornbusch, comp., *Military Bibliography of the Civil War*, 2 vols. (New York: New York Public Library, 1961–1967; reprint 1971–1972); *Civil War Regiments: A Journal of the American Civil War* (Campbell, Calif: Savas Publishing); Alwyn Barr, "An Essay on Texas Civil War Historiography," in *Texas, the Dark Corner of the Confederacy: Contemporary Accounts of the Lone Star State in the Civil War*, ed. B. P. Gallaway, 3d ed. (Lincoln: University of Nebraska Press, 1994), 257–76.

with a growing recognition that soldiers as well as generals shaped the war.[2]

The history in *Polignac's Texas Brigade* offers readers the opportunity to understand the members of a less well known unit and their roles in several battles west of the Mississippi River. With this further knowledge, the reader can better comprehend factors that at times dampened the soldiers' morale: mixed feelings about secession, extensive illness, frustrations over conversion from cavalry to infantry, harsh weather conditions, changes in commanders, and reluctance about orders given late in the war to cross the Mississippi and serve farther from home. The complexity of the Civil War becomes more apparent as one marches in the shoes or boots of these soldiers.

Since *Polignac's Texas Brigade* first appeared, other accounts have been published with a focus on one of the regiments or companies in the larger unit. Others have presented the memoirs or letters of an individual soldier. Each adds important information to flesh out the history of the brigade.

Three new accounts focus on the 34th Texas Cavalry. The most extensive is by Robert S. Weddle, *Plow-horse Cavalry: The Caney Creek Boys of the Thirty-fourth Texas*. Developing a narrative around letters to and from his grandfather, A. L. Nelms, Weddle follows the North Texas regiment through its successes and problems from 1862 to 1865. The focus of the book shifts when, in 1864, Nelms began serving apart from the regiment. Another narrative by a member of the 34th Texas is John Calvin Williams's "A Rebel Remembers the Red River Campaign." Writing in 1900 with some sense of humor, Williams described his service throughout the conflict, including time as a prisoner of war in 1864. The views of a third member of the 34th Texas appear in J. S. Duncan's "A Soldier's Fare is Rough: Letters from A. Cameron in the Indian Territory, Arkansas Campaign, 1862–1864."[3]

---

[2] See Richard E. Beringer, Herman Hattaway, Archer Jones, and William N. Still, Jr., *Why the South Lost the Civil War* (Athens: University of Georgia Press, 1986).

[3] Weddle, (Austin, Tex.: Madrona Press, 1974); Williams, *Civil War Times Illustrated* 17 (January 1979): 20–31; Duncan, *Military History of Texas and the Southwest* 12, no. 1 (1975): 39–61.

The 31st Texas Cavalry is the focus of two new narratives. Cameron changed regiments within the brigade to become a lieutenant in the 31st Texas. His later service is described by J. S. Duncan in "Alexander Cameron in the Louisiana Campaign, 1863–1865." Douglas V. Mead, in *Texas Wanderlust: The Adventures of Dutch Wurzbach*, builds upon the memoirs of his great-grandfather, Emil F. Wurzbach, to discuss service with the 31st Texas. The description of the skirmish at Vidalia, Louisiana, differs from other versions. Illness forced Wurzbach to return home in 1864.[4]

Two new studies consider the 15th Texas Infantry. In *Parson Henry Renfro: Free Thinking on the Texas Frontier*, William Clark Griggs explores the life of his great-great-grandfather, using family correspondence of the period. Renfro, a Baptist minister, became chaplain of the 15th Texas during its time in Louisiana from 1863 to 1865. Andrew L. Leath has published the rolls of two companies in the 15th Texas regiment.[5]

The 17th Texas Consolidated Regiment is the focus of three new accounts. Douglas Hale, in "One Man's War: Captain Joseph H. Bruton, 1861–1865," narrates events during 1864, based primarily on Bruton's letters. Another account by a member of that unit, for the same period, is Norman C. Delaney's "The Diary and Memoirs of Marshall Samuel Pierson, Company C, 17th Regiment, Texas Cavalry, 1862–1865." Leath also has published the roll of a company in the 17th Texas.[6]

Two new narratives are devoted to the 11th Texas Battalion. W. T. Block discusses "The Swamp Angels: A History of Spaight's 11th Battalion, Texas Volunteers, CSA," including their service with the brigade in Louisiana during 1863. A briefer account, "Spaight's Bat-

[4] Duncan, *Military History of Texas and the Southwest* 12, no. 4 (1975): 245–71 and vol. 13, no. 1 (1976): 37–57; Mead, (College Station: Texas A&M University Press, 1997).

[5] Griggs, (Austin: University of Texas Press, 1994); Leath, *Chronicles of Smith County, Texas* 32 (summer 1993): 8–12 and vol. 33 (winter 1994): 11–15.

[6] Hale, *East Texas Historical Journal* 20, no. 2 (1982): 28–45; Delaney, *Military History of Texas and the Southwest* 13, no. 3 (1976): 23–38; Leath, *Chronicles of Smith County, Texas* 34 (winter 1996): 11–14.

talion, CSA," by Charles Ray Walker, includes rolls for all six companies.[7]

Commanders of Polignac's brigade have received further attention in recent years. Polignac himself is the subject of "The Prince and the Confederates," by Roy O. Hatton. *Acadian General Alfred Mouton and the Civil War*, by William Arceneaux, is a biography of the officer who led the infantry division in Louisiana that included Polignac's brigade. That division, and others, served under the army commander described by T. Michael Parrish in *Richard Taylor: Soldier Prince of Dixie*.[8]

Two books expand our knowledge and understanding of Unionists in Texas during the Civil War period. Richard B. McCaslin offers a thoughtful view of events in North Texas in *Tainted Breeze: The Great Hanging at Gainesville, Texas, 1862*. A wider geographical view of the topic is *Texas Divided: Loyalty and Dissent in the Lone Star State, 1856–1874*, by James Marten. To place the service of Polignac's brigade in broader perspective one should see: Ralph A. Wooster, *Texas and Texans in the Civil War*, and Robert L. Kerby, *Kirby Smith's Confederacy: The Trans-Mississippi South, 1863–1865*.[9]

---

[7] Block, *East Texas Historical Journal* 30, no. 1 (1992): 44–57; Walker, *Texas Gulf Historical and Biographical Record* 8 (November 1972): 22–38.

[8] *Civil War Times Illustrated* 19 (August 1980): 8–13; Arceneaux, (Lafayette, La.: University of Southwestern Louisiana, 1972); Parrish, (Chapel Hill: University of North Carolina Press, 1992).

[9] McCaslin, (Baton Rouge: Louisiana State University Press, 1994); Marten, (Lexington: University Press of Kentucky, 1990); Wooster, (Austin, Tex.: Eakin Press, 1995); Kerby, (New York: Columbia University Press, 1972).

# Preface to the First Edition

This study began with the discovery of a series of letters from James E. Harrison to William Pitt Ballinger, during the period 1861–1865, among the Ballinger Papers in the Archives of the University of Texas Library. It soon became evident from additional research that the letters, written by a ranking Texas officer in the Trans-Mississippi theatre of the Civil War, provided detailed information about a brigade of Texans which had almost disappeared from the history of that great conflict. Continued investigation revealed some rare and even unique features in the story of Polignac's Texas Brigade. Much of the brigade was recruited from the partially Unionist inhabitants of North Texas, who held many different views on the war and generally lacked the war spirit found in most other portions of the state. Three regiments were raised as cavalry and later dismounted to serve as infantry; another was a consolidated command composed of Texans who had escaped from the capture of Arkansas Post in 1863. Finally, in 1863, the brigade received as its commander the only foreign citizen to become a Confederate general, Prince Camille de Polignac. This oddly assorted unit served under ten commanders, in ten major engagements, and through long periods of skirmishing and hardship in Missouri, Arkansas, the Indian Territory, Louisiana, and Texas.

Yet the members of this command, which at various times included approximately five thousand men, left virtually no printed records of their service. Perhaps, as Lester N. Fitzhugh has suggested, the Confederates of the Trans-Mississippi said and wrote little of their experiences, because all too often they were silenced by comparisons with the experiences of men who had fought in the Army of Northern Virginia or in the Army of Tennessee. For that reason, there have been included in this study several lengthy quotations from unpublished manuscripts which provide detailed accounts of previously obscure Confederate movements in a number of battles and campaigns. Although the men of Polignac's brigade served in secondary campaigns with a limited effect on the outcome of the conflict, they were very much a part of the American Civil War, and a factor in those events which took place west of the Mississippi River.

The analogies to war in general that may be drawn from this study are not new. They are present in every realistic account of any war. For basically war between or within nations is the result of men's inability or refusal to understand, respect, and attempt to compromise their own interests with those of others. There may be many variations of opinion as to what are the interests of a nation or a section, as there were in the United States, the South, and Texas in 1861. But once war begins, everyone within the opposing nations or sections is involved in some way, on one side or the other, with or without his consent. Thus men at war are often united or divided only by the instinct to survive. Under such conditions, selfless acts of perseverance and courage are worthy of admiration; but they should never cause anyone to forget that the overall effects of war are suffering, destruction, death, and the brutalization of men. War is indeed hell for most of those involved.

This then is not the story of another all-victorious command of superb fighting men, or of another band of heroes defeated by fantastic odds. Fewer of these commands exist in actual combat than are found in the pages of history books. This is an account of the widely varied experiences of some men, Texans, in the army of the Confederate States of America.

The history of Polignac's Texas Brigade was pieced together with the guidance and assistance of Professor Barnes F. Lathrop of the University of Texas; Mr. Chester V. Kielman and Mr. Charles W. Corkran of the Archives, University of Texas Library; Professor Guy Bryan Harrison, Jr., of Baylor University; Mr. Cooper K. Ragan of Houston, Texas; Mr. R. Henderson Shuffler of the Humanities Research Center, University of Texas; Mr. Robert S. Weddle of Menard, Texas; Mr. James M. Day of the Archives, Texas State Library; Judge Lester Newton Fitzhugh of Lancaster, Texas; Miss Katherine Bridges of the Russell Library, Northwestern State College of Louisiana; Mr. Roy Hatton of Baton Rouge, Louisiana; Mr. A. H. Plummer of the Mansfield Battle Park Museum, Mansfield, Louisiana; Mrs. C.

B. Tate of Austin, Texas; Mrs. N. W. Jenkins of Mansfield, Louisiana; Mr. Llewellyn Notley of Teague, Texas; Mr. Robert W. Glover of Tyler Junior College; Mr. Robert E. Davis of Waco, Texas; Frances V. Parker of Austin, Texas; and my wife Nancy. I wish to express my appreciation to them, and also to the Texas Gulf Coast Historical Association for publishing this study.

Polignac's Texas Brigade

Chapter I

# "Our trail was a long graveyard"

# Arkansas, Missouri, and the Indian Territory, 1862-1863

In late July, 1862, three Texas cavalry regiments were loosely brigaded for the first time, along with some Indian regiments, under Colonel Douglas H. Cooper near Fort Smith, Arkansas. For the next three years, mounted and dismounted, through the numbing cold of winter snow and the sultry summer heat of swamps, the 22nd Texas Cavalry, the 31st Texas Cavalry, and the 34th Texas Cavalry formed the nucleus of a Confederate brigade which fought from Missouri to Louisiana in defense of the Trans-Mississippi Department. In the summer of 1862, however, all three were still raw regiments, none having been in combat during its three to six months of service.

The 22nd Texas Cavalry had been recruited in Fannin, Grayson, Collin, and surrounding counties of North Texas during the winter of 1861-1862. Robert H. Taylor, a prominent lawyer and former member of the Texas legislature from Bonham, raised the regiment and became its first colonel. Thirty-six years old in 1861, Taylor had commanded a company of Texas Rangers under John C. Hays in the Mexican War and had opposed secession until the Civil War began. As lieutenant colonel the Texans chose William H. Johnson of Paris, an Alabama-born lawyer and former state legislator. Johnson was best known as one of the eight members of the Texas Secession Convention who voted against the secession ordinance. James G. Stevens, a tall, dark-haired, thirty-eight year old, Alabama-born trader from Hunt County, had been elected major.[1]

---

[1] Bob Taylor to Ben [H. Epperson], November 20, 1861, Benjamin H. Epperson Collection, Archives, University of Texas Library; Clarksville *Standard*, September 6, 1856, December 21, 1861; Dallas *Herald*, January 8, 29, 1862; Ernest W. Winkler, ed., *Journal of the Secession Convention of Texas, 1861* (Austin, 1912), 49, 406; William DeRyee and R. E. Moore, comps., *The Texas Album of the Eighth Legislature, 1860* (Austin, 1860), 178; *Members of the Legislature of the State of Texas from 1846 to 1939* (Austin, 1939), 15, 20, 35; Ralph A. Wooster, "Analysis of the Membership of the Texas Secession Convention," *Southwestern Historical Quarterly*, LXII, 332; James G. Stevens Carded File, War Department Collection of Confederate Records, National Archives.

At Fort Washita in the Indian Territory, on January 16, 1862, the 22nd Texas Cavalry had been organized "for 12 months to serve between Kansas and Texas" occupying the former Federal outposts north of the Red River. Illusions of light service close to home ended quickly with an order from Colonel Cooper for the Texans to reinforce his Confederate command on the North Fork of the Canadian River defending the Indian Territory against invasion from the north. There, in the spring of 1862, Taylor's regiment was joined by the 34th Texas Cavalry.[2]

Men from North Texas also made up the 34th Texas Cavalry, with companies representing an area bordering the Indian Territory from Cooke County to Red River County and extending south and west to Erath and Palo Pinto counties. Recruiting for the unit had been conducted during the winter of 1861-1862. In February, 1862, the regiment had been completed in the Indian Territory with Almerine M. Alexander, a forty-two year old Kentucky-born merchant of Sherman and Bonham as colonel, George H. Wooten as lieutenant colonel, and John R. Russell, a Bonham merchant and Mexican War veteran originally from North Carolina, as major. Among the captains of the regiment was William M. Bush of Company G, Collin County, a Mexican War veteran originally from Kentucky. Official organization took place on April 17, 1862.[3]

Neither the 22nd nor the 34th Texas had been raised with the war spirit prevalent in units from East and Central Texas. Men comprising both regiments came primarily from the northern border counties of Texas. A majority of the population of that area in turn had come from the upper South or from border states, included few slaveholders, and had little voice in state politics. Rep-

---

[2] Taylor to Ben, November 20, 1861, Epperson Collection; Douglas H. Cooper to Albert Pike, February 10, 1862, War of the Rebellion: A Compilation of the Official Records of the Union and Confederate Armies (70 vols. in 128; Washington, 1880-1901), Series I, Vol. XIII, 896; Pike to Sir, May 4, 1862, ibid., 821; List of Military Organizations Carded by the Record and Pension Office, Confederate, Texas Lists, 1-241, Record Group No. 94, National Archives, photostat, Archives, Texas State Library, 40.

[3] Ibid., 53; Muster Roll, Company G, 34th Texas Dismounted Cavalry, June 30, 1863, photostat, Archives, University of Texas Library, original in National Archives, Washington, D.C.; U. S. Eighth Census, 1860, Returns of Schedule 1, Free Inhabitants, for Grayson County, Texas, microfilm, University of Texas Library, 25; Clarksville Standard, March 1, 1862; Dallas Herald, August 19, 1865; Dudley G. Wooten, ed., Comprehensive History of Texas, 1685-1897 (2 vols.; Dallas, 1898), II, 639-640; Biographical Souvenir of the State of Texas (Chicago, 1889), 138; Walter H. Bush, "Maj. William M. Bush," Confederate Veteran, VIII, 546-547; J. Lee and Lillian J. Stambaugh, A History of Collin County, Texas (Austin, 1958), 268-270; Graham Landrum, Grayson County, An Illustrated History of Grayson County, Texas (Fort Worth, 1960), 21-22, 26, 60; R. M. Lusk, Constantine Lodge No. 13 Ancient, Free and Accepted Masons (Bonham, 1917), 37.

resentatives of the North Texas area cast five of the eight votes against the Texas ordinance of secession in the convention of 1861. When the ordinance later was submitted to the people for ratification, eight of the nineteen counties which opposed secession lay in North Texas.[4] Although many different views had existed in North Texas in 1861, opinion in general resembled that found in the upper South and in the border states, where a majority had been sympathetic to the lower South but opposed to secession. Robert H. Taylor expressed those views with courage and foresight in the Texas House of Representatives in January, 1861, when he spoke against recognizing the Texas Secession Convention, saying "We are in the midst of Revolution, and he who can check its progress or direct its course, so as to avoid its consequences upon the people, will indeed merit the applause of his countrymen." He branded secession "this unholy scheme to destroy the best government under the sun." But he continued, "I want my people to wake up, think for themselves, . . . and when they shall have spoken fairly at the ballot box, I am with them through good or evil report, and then this good right arm, which has never refused its country's call, shall be among the first to repel foreign invasion or domestic violence."[5] As in the upper South, only Fort Sumter and Lincoln's call for troops had placed a majority of North Texans behind the Confederate government. Taylor probably expressed their views again, when he wrote to Ben Epperson in the fall of 1861, that the war "is upon us. Let us help to fight it out. Then in the future no one can say that we led the opposition to secession and then stood by and said the country go to the Devil without staying the tide of war."[6]

By May, 1862, both regiments reached Fort McCulloch in the Indian Territory where only 829 men were reported present out of 1,679 on their rolls. The great disparity stemmed from a variety of causes. There had been excessive sickness among the Texans who were still new to army life. Also numerous furloughs had been granted to farmers to harvest an early wheat crop. In addition, most of the Texans were "originally Union men, and raised under

---

[4] Floyd F. Ewing, Jr., "Origins of Unionist Sentiment on the West Texas Frontier," *West Texas Historical Association Year Book*, XXXII, 21-29; Floyd F. Ewing, Jr., "Unionist Sentiment on the Northwest Texas Frontier," *ibid.*, XXXIII, 58-70; Winkler, *Journal of the Secession Convention of Texas, 1861*, pp. 49, 88-90.

[5] Speech of Robert H. Taylor, delivered in the House of Representatives, . . . upon the joint resolutions, to recognize or approve the Convention to assemble 28th of January, 1861, Broadside, Archives, University of Texas Library.

[6] Taylor to Ben, November 20, 1861, Epperson Collection.

express promise that they should be stationed on the frontier at Forts Washita and Arbuckle, and not required to go elsewhere to serve."

In June, the two regiments were placed on standby orders for a march into Arkansas to reinforce Major General Thomas C. Hindman, the new district commander. The orders were a result of Hindman's efforts to defend Arkansas against an expected Federal invasion from southern Missouri, which had been under Union control since the Confederate defeat at Pea Ridge in northwestern Arkansas during March. Instead, the Texans whiled away time in unit reorganization and in construction of fortifications to their openly avowed displeasure. The feeling had been mutual with the eccentric commander of the Indian Territory, Brigadier General Albert Pike, who felt that his poorly disciplined Texas cavalry were "even more worthless and troublesome together than I supposed."[7] Actually the Texans were caught in the midst of a bitter feud over troop allocations between Pike and his superior, Hindman, which resulted in Pike's resignation in mid-July, 1862.[8] Finally on July 8, the call came and later that month both regiments, in groups of battalion strength, moved slowly toward Fort Smith through the drought stricken Indian Territory.[9]

Brigade organization came after the arrival of the 31st Texas Cavalry. Colonel Trezevant C. Hawpe, a forty year old Dallas businessman and former city and county official, had raised the 31st Texas primarily in Dallas County and the surrounding area in North Texas. "Who Will Defend Texas, Texans and Texans Alone" read Hawpe's advertisement for troops in a January, 1862, issue of the Dallas *Herald*. The response to this and other notices by would-be company commanders had been steady if not overwhelming, and on May 15 the regiment was organized in Dallas with enlistments "For the war." Exceptions to the North Texas

---

[7] Albert Pike to President Davis, July 31, 1862, *Official Records*, Series I, Vol. XIII, 865-866; Abstract from Return of the Department of Indian Territory for May, 1862, *ibid.*, 831; Pike to J. S. Roane, June 1, 1862, *ibid.*, 935-936; Pike to T. C. Hindman, July 3, 1862, *ibid.*, 956-957; List of Military Organizations Carded by the Record and Pension Office, Confederate, Texas Lists, 1-241, Record Group No. 94, National Archives, photostat, Archives, Texas State Library, 40, 53.

[8] Ezra J. Warner, *Generals in Gray: Lives of the Confederate Commanders* (Baton Rouge, 1959), 240.

[9] Albert Pike to Major General Hindman, July 15, 1862, *Official Records*, Series I, Vol. XIII, 857; Pike to The Secretary of War, July 20, 1862, *ibid.*, 859; A. L. Nelms to M. J. Nelms, July 19, 1862, Montee Nelms Weddle Collection, Archives, University of Texas Library.

predominance were Companies C and F from Bexar and Travis counties.[10]

George W. Guess, a Dallas attorney and alderman, who originally enlisted as a private in the Dallas Light Artillery in 1861, became lieutenant colonel of the regiment. Frederick J. Malone, a graduate of the University of Mississippi and a Mexican War veteran, was chosen major. Each had been active in raising troops, the most important attribute for prospective officers at election time, even in place of prior experience.[11]

Nine companies had been mustered from early March until mid-May. Their strength varied from seventy-eight to forty-nine men, and all companies accepted additional recruits wherever men could be found and persuaded to enlist. Age ranged widely with fifteen and forty-nine being the admitted extremes. Most men brought horses but few were well armed, and Hawpe had been forced to request weapons from the citizens of Dallas to arm his troops.[12]

On May 17, the regiment and citizens of Dallas combined to enjoy a picnic at the camp of Company A, Captain William W. Peak's recruits from Dallas. A holiday air prevailed as the company drilled for its assembled well wishers. At least one observer detected a melancholy undercurrent among those present, however, stimulated no doubt by thoughts of leaving home to face the great unknown of war.[13]

Hawpe set his men in motion for Little Rock during the first week in June, 1862, and they were all on the road north by June 12. The regiment rode casually across North Texas through Paris and Clarksville under command of Lieutenant Colonel Guess. Hawpe in the meantime made a personal visit to Brigadier General Henry E. McCulloch in Tyler to collect his men's bounty pay for

[10] Confederate Muster Rolls Nos. 1131, 1177, 1186, 1213, 1271, 1542, Archives, Texas State Library; Muster Rolls, Company C, 31st Texas Cavalry, Henry W. Dailey Collection, Archives, University of Texas Library; Wooten, *Comprehensive History of Texas, 1685-1897*, II, 637-638; *Memorial and Biographical History of Dallas County, Texas* (Chicago, 1892), 799; John Henry Brown, *History of Dallas County, Texas, From 1837 to 1887* (Dallas, 1887), 24, 25; John H. Cochran, *Dallas County: A Record of Its Pioneers and Progress* . . . (Dallas, 1928), 90-92; Dallas *Herald*, January 15, February 12, May 17, 1862.

[11] *Ibid.*, August 19, 1863; Monroe F. Cockrell, Preface, Civil War Letters, Guess to Cockrell, Archives, University of Texas Library; L. E. Daniell, *Personnel of the Texas State Government, with Sketches of Representative Men of Texas* (San Antonio, 1892), 486-487; Brown, *History of Dallas County*, 53.

[12] Confederate Muster Rolls Nos. 1131, 1177, 1186, 1213, 1271, 1542, Archives, Texas State Library; Muster Rolls, Company C, 31st Texas Cavalry, Dailey Collection; Dallas *Herald*, May 31, 1862.

[13] *Ibid.*, May 24, 1862.

enlistment. The funds were distributed at "Camp Bounty" in Bowie County, and on July 5, 1862, the 31st Texas crossed the Red River into Arkansas. McCulloch also provided money for forage and provisions, but all excess baggage and wagons had been left behind in a forced march to reinforce Hindman at his order. Despite rain and a shortage of coats and tents the regiment arrived in Little Rock on July 18 in good spirits. From there Hindman sent Hawpe's troopers to the neighborhood of Fort Smith, where the 22nd and the 34th Texas awaited them under Colonel D. H. Cooper, a former Indian agent, whose military reputation rested on his service as a captain in the 1st Mississippi Rifles during the Mexican War.[14]

The mountainous area on the border of Arkansas and the Indian Territory apparently created health problems for the 31st Texas as it lay in camp around Fort Smith. While the newly arrived Texans fought sickness, the 34th Texas moved its camp in the Indian Territory north from Fort Gibson to Park Hill where the cavalrymen skirmished with Union Indians. A short period allowed for rest, the collection of provisions, and the repair of weapons passed quickly, then Cooper led his men north toward the Missouri line. At Camp Osage south of Bentonville, Arkansas, the brigade halted temporarily to recover from a siege of measles which put eighty-eight men in the hospital at one time in late August. Colonel Joseph Shelby joined the Texans on August 28 with a brigade of Missouri cavalry and the combined commands moved into Missouri in September, 1862. Fall weather in the mountains made the Texans mindful of winter and officers were sent home to collect clothes for the approaching cold season.[15]

Confederate forays into Union-held areas in Missouri began almost immediately, and Cooper's Texans met Federals for the first time on September 20, 1862. At eight o'clock that morning detachments of the 31st and the 34th Texas drove in the pickets of a Union Indian regiment at Shirley's Ford on Spring River west of Carthage, Missouri. Hawpe's and Alexander's horsemen stampeded a group of civilians camped with the Federal unit for protection, captured some stores, and burned others before the Union commander could organize his defenses. A farther advance was halted by Federal infantry concealed in a ravine, and the Texans withdrew before a

---

[14] *Ibid.*, June 7, 14, 21, July 5, August 2, 1862; Warner, *Generals in Gray*, 61-62; George W. Guess to Mrs. Sarah H. Cockrell, June 26, 29, July 17, 1862, February 8, 1863, Civil War Letters, Guess to Cockrell, photostats, Archives, University of Texas Library. All succeeding citations of Guess or Cockrell correspondence will refer to this collection.

[15] George W. Guess to Mrs. Sarah H. Cockrell, July 29, 1862; A. L. Nelms to M. J. Nelms, August 3, 18, September 12, 1862, Weddle Collection; Dallas *Herald*, August 16, September 6, 20, October 4, 1862.

combined cavalry-infantry counterattack. Confederate losses totaled twenty killed and wounded, while Union losses included nine wounded and twelve to twenty killed.[16]

On September 24, Cooper's brigade camped at Scott's Mill, then rode on to reunite with Shelby at Big Spring on Indian Creek during the 26th. Cooper sent Hawpe's 31st Texas and an Indian battalion to Newtonia, five miles to the north, as an advanced post on September 27. Rumors of a Federal advance from Sarcoxie, Missouri, toward Granby on the 28th drew out Confederate patrols but they detected little activity in any direction. Next morning, however, Hawpe's pickets were engaged by Union skirmishers along the Granby road. Cooper sent reinforcements to Newtonia from Camp Coffee on Indian Creek and ordered the 22nd Texas to Granby under its recently promoted colonel, James G. Stevens. The Missouri troops at Newtonia fell back to Camp Coffee on the morning of September 30 and Alexander's 34th Texas marched for Granby to relieve Stevens' men.

Union skirmishers appeared from the west and northwest less than an hour after Cooper left Newtonia to the care of the 31st Texas and a single field battery. Hawpe placed his men dismounted behind a stone wall and again called for reinforcements. Cooper arrived with the 34th Texas and sent them to the right below a mill where they dismounted to fight on foot. Alexander's men were soon ordered to remount, however, and they retired behind the stone wall to Hawpe's right. With the approach of support there also had come confusion, and out of the confusion had come a mistaken order for the 31st Texas to counterattack. Over the wall spilled the dismounted cavalrymen into a ragged charge, which was forced back by Federal artillery fire. Suddenly Stevens' regiment galloped onto the field with two Indian battalions, striking the Union right in a column of platoons. The Federal line wavered, than retreated under the steady pressure of Stevens' charge which swept up eighty prisoners in a four mile pursuit.

Fighting lapsed for a time around noon and scouts from the 22nd Texas were sent forward to determine enemy intentions. The reinforced Union command under Brigadier General Frederick S. Salomon returned to the attack early in the afternoon. Fighting men again struggled for the stone wall and the fields on either side of the village while a Federal column tried to turn the Confederate right. Meanwhile Cooper continued to bring for-

---

[16] *Ibid.*, October 11, 1862; Wooten, *Comprehensive History of Texas, 1685-1897*, II, 640; report of John Ritchie, September 21, 1862, *Official Records*, Series I, Vol. XIII, 277-278; Ritchie to James G. Blunt, September 23, 1862, *ibid.*, 661.

ward Southern reinforcements until his entire force was concentrated in and around Newtonia by 5:00 P.M. Then he ordered an advance by all units. The 31st Texas was on the left, the 34th Texas formed part of the center, and the 22nd Texas was with the left in the Confederate charge which cleared the field of Union troops by dark. Losses among the Texans were one killed, thirty-one wounded, and one missing out of seventy-eight Southern casualties.[17] All three regiments had borne their part in the Confederate victory with tenacity and courage.

On October 3, Cooper received word that Major General John M. Schofield, commanding all Union forces in southwest Missouri, was pressing rapidly toward Newtonia to redeem the defeat of his advance units. Shelby formed the troops at Newtonia in line of battle on the 4th with the 31st Texas in the center and the 34th Texas on the right. The Federals were forced to deploy for action allowing Shelby time to organize his retreat along the road to Pineville. Some confusion resulted as the Confederates began to withdraw and Alexander was momentarily unaware that a retreat had begun. He rejoined the main body quickly, however, as did the 22nd Texas which had marched for the front, along with some Indian units, under Cooper from Camp Coffee. Stevens' troops also were cut off for a short time but found the Confederate column and served as a rear guard until relieved by two Missouri regiments near Pineville. On October 5, detachments of the 34th and the 22nd Texas again resumed rear guard duties.[18]

The retreat continued into northwestern Arkansas where Cooper and the Indian units were separated from the Texans and ordered into the Indian Territory on October 15. In the meantime, there had been added to the brigade the 20th Texas Cavalry, commanded by Colonel Thomas Coke Bass, a prewar lawyer and ardent secessionist who had come to Texas from Mississippi. Suddenly at Holcombe, Arkansas, on October 16, Bass became brigade commander by seniority despite his lack of combat experience. The retreat and change in command had helped disorganize the brigade which already had been hard hit by sickness and probably

---

[17] Report of Douglas H. Cooper, October 2, 1862, *ibid.*, 296-300; report of T. C. Hawpe, . . . , 1862, *ibid.*, 305-306; report of A. M. Alexander, October 13, 1862, *ibid.*, 306-307; report of J. G. Stevens, October 13, 1862, *ibid.*, 303-305; Return of Casualties in Cooper's division, Newtonia, September 30, 1862, *ibid.*, 301; John N. Edwards, *Shelby and His Men, or The War in the West* (Cincinnati, 1867), 87-88. The Dallas *Herald*, November 15, 1862, reported the Texan losses at Newtonia as three killed, twenty-seven wounded, and two missing.

[18] Report of Douglas H. Cooper, December 15, 1862, *Official Records*, Series I, Vol. XIII, 333-334; report of A. M. Alexander, October 13, 1862, *ibid.*, 306-307; report of J. G. Stevens, October 13, 1862, *ibid.*, 304-305.

by war-weariness among many of those who had originally opposed secession. Because Bass obviously was not the man to restore order, Hindman sent Colonel William R. Bradfute, one of his staff officers, to take command of the brigade and resist the Federal advance. Bradfute, a Mexican War veteran from Tennessee, was known to some of the Texans through his service on the Texas frontier as a captain in the 2nd United States Cavalry during the 1850's. The brigade became part of Brigadier General James S. Rains' division, but confusion increased as the retreat continued. Rains resigned after having been drunk on duty, while Stevens and Bass were arrested for retreating without cause. Hindman then placed the Texans in Brigadier General John S. Marmaduke's division, but the change proved to be no cure for their lagging morale and discipline. Bradfute soon fell ill and relinquished command of the brigade without reporting the fact to Hindman. After another brief moment of confusion Colonel Jesse L. Craven was made temporary brigade commander and the men's over-all behavior improved noticeably.

The improvement came too late to save the Texans from a fate feared by all cavalrymen. Hindman's patience had worn out. He felt the Texas regiments were "worthless as cavalry, and . . . ordered them dismounted and their ponies sent to Texas" on November 1, 1862.[19] In addition, he requested permission to consolidate the four regiments into two because straggling and sickness had severely limited their size, but the petition apparently went unheeded. The Texans trudged south with aching feet and hurt pride, which produced long standing bitter resentment toward Hindman and further demoralized the ex-cavalrymen.[20]

As infantry the four regiments, again under Bradfute, became part of Brigadier General John S. Roane's command at Van Buren during the first week in November, 1862. Wagons with winter clothes arrived from Texas later in the month and morale among the Texans improved to some extent in spite of dismounting, no pay, and rations of parched corn. Lieutenant Colonel John R. Russell of the 34th Texas resigned because of ill health at the end of November, however, while M. W. Davenport became

---

19 Report of Thomas C. Hindman, November 3, 1862, *ibid.*, 47-48; D. D. Whetston Day Book, November 1, 1862, Dailey Collection; Dallas *Herald*, November 15, 1862; Landrum, *Grayson County*, 122; H. L. Bentley and Thomas Pilgrim, *The Texas Legal Directory for 1876-77* (Austin, 1877), 41; Francis B. Heitman, *Historical Register and Dictionary of the United States Army, from its Organization, September 29, 1789 to March 2, 1903* (2 vols.; Washington, 1903), I, 238.

20 George W. Guess to Mrs. Sarah H. Cockrell, November 30, 1862.

major of the regiment replacing Sevier Tackett who had died of typhoid earlier in the fall.[21]

Early in December, Hindman began a limited offensive aimed at crushing Major General James G. Blunt's Federal division in northwestern Arkansas before reinforcements could arrive from Missouri. Brigadier General Francis J. Herron, Union commander in Springfield, Missouri, learned of the Confederate advance, however, and pressed south through Fayetteville to support Blunt. Hindman then feinted west at Blunt and turned east to attack Herron on December 7. But the initiative was lost when Brigadier General Francis A. Shoup, commanding Hindman's lead infantry division, halted in a defensive position at Prairie Grove.

Throughout the morning of December 7, Shoup and the Confederate cavalry held off Herron. Brigadier General Daniel M. Frost's division, which included Roane's command made up primarily of the Texas regiments, was held in reserve to meet Blunt's division when it arrived on the field. The second Federal command approached at about 2:00 P.M. and formed 2,000 yards from Shoup's left for an assault on the visible Confederate line. Frost's division then advanced through woods filled with thick undergrowth to extend the Southern left flank. There the Texans helped beat off three Union attacks, following up each time with a counterattack to the edge of the timber.[22] Lieutenant Colonel Guess, commanding the 31st Texas, summarized the situation with the statement that

> Our Brig[ade] was posted on the extreme left w[ing] of the army and was not called into prominent action but a short time, but not a boy or man of them showed any disposition to flinch. The cannon balls and shells flew and burst around them and the minnie [sic] ball whistled about their ears, but they stood calm and determined to die or win the victory.[23]

Artillery fire set hay stacks in adjoining fields ablaze, resulting in terrible burns for wounded who had taken shelter in them. Cries from the wounded mingled with the subsiding sounds of battle to end the day upon a truly grotesque note. When night came the Confederates had retained their position against every

---

[21] *Ibid.;* A. L. Nelms to M. J. Nelms, November 5, December 1, 1862, Weddle Collection; Wooten, *Comprehensive History of Texas, 1685-1897,* II, 638; M. L. Bell to Brigadier General Marmaduke, November 9, 1862, *Official Records,* Series I, Vol. XIII, 912.

[22] Organization of the Army of the Trans-Mississippi Department, December 12, 1862, *ibid.,* Series I, Vol. XXII, Pt. 1, 903; report of Thomas C. Hindman, December 25, 1862, *ibid.,* 138-142; report of James G. Blunt, December 20, 1862, *ibid.,* 74-76; Wooten, *Comprehensive History of Texas, 1685-1897,* II, 638, 640; Charles W. Walker, "Battle of Prairie Grove," *Publications of the Arkansas Historical Association,* II, 355.

[23] George W. Guess to Mrs. S. H. Cockrell, December 16, 1862.

assault, but lack of ammunition for the next day forced Hindman to retire from the field. Casualties in the Texas brigade were not reported, except for Captain John Duncan of the 31st Texas who lost a leg as the result of a wound at Prairie Grove.

The retreat carried the Texas brigade back to the Arkansas River near Fort Smith. There in late December, morale fell to a new low and numerous desertions followed a near mutiny in the 31st Texas when Bradfute ordered a man punished by bucking. Then in early January, 1863, came orders for a march to Little Rock. Near Clarksville, Arkansas, the dismounted cavalrymen were halted and the brigade was reorganized with the addition of the fresh, untested 15th Texas Infantry from Brigadier General Henry E. McCulloch's division near Little Rock.[24]

Texans in the 15th Texas Infantry had been recruited primarily around Waco in Central Texas and at Millican near Houston for the 1st Battalion Texas Infantry, organized with six companies on February 18, 1862. In a three-way shuffle during April, four of the battalion's original companies were combined into three and transferred to the 1st Regiment Texas Heavy Artillery. They had been replaced by three companies from the 13th Texas Infantry, which had been recruited at Velasco on the Gulf Coast and at Corsicana in East Texas. The 15th Texas Infantry had been filled out that spring, while additions to company rolls were made on the march through East Texas to Arkansas in June and July.[25] For his efforts in raising the regiment, Joseph Warren Speight, a thirty-six year old North Carolina-born lawyer-planter of Waco, was chosen colonel. The rank of lieutenant colonel went to James E. Harrison of Waco, a former Texas Indian commissioner and Mississippi state senator originally from South Carolina. John W. Daniel of Smith County, a thirty-one year old farmer born in Virginia, had been elected major at Millican. The regimental adjutant was John B. Jones, a small soft-spoken South Carolina-born planter who was to achieve renown as a major in the postwar Texas Rangers and as Adjutant General of Texas. David R. Wallace, the regimental surgeon, originally from North Carolina, had

---

[24] A. L. Nelms to M. J. Nelms, December 24, 1862, Weddle Collection; Edwards, *Shelby and His Men*, 131; Wooten, *Comprehensive History of Texas, 1685-1897*, II, 638-639.

[25] Muster Rolls, Companies A, B, C, D, E, F, G, H, I, 15th Texas Infantry, Texas History Collection, Baylor University; List of Military Organizations Carded by the Record and Pension Office, Confederate, Texas Lists, 1-241, Record Group No. 94, National Archives, photostat, Archives, Texas State Library; James Allen Hamilton Diary, October 4, 1861 - April 13, 1862, Archives, University of Texas Library; James E. Harrison to Dear [William Pitt] Ballinger, January 3, 11, April 25, 26, 1862, Ballinger Collection, Archives, University of Texas Library.

graduated from Wake Forest College and New York University, and would later become president of the Texas State Medical Association in the 1870's. Among the original company commanders were George B. Erath, a frontier Indian fighter and former member of the Texas legislature, and Richard Coke, a young Virginia-born law graduate of William and Mary College, who represented Waco in the Texas Secession Convention. Coke was to become governor of Texas from 1874 to 1876 and thereafter was to serve in the United States Senate until 1895.[26]

Farmers constituted a large majority of the infantrymen in the 15th Texas. A hodgepodge of teachers, druggists, printers, tailors, carpenters, coopers, clerks, stage drivers, stockmen, shoemakers, bricklayers, blacksmiths, barbers, millers, merchants, mechanics, tinners, tanners, teamsters, an engineer, a hunter, and a carriage maker filled out the remainder of the regiment. Each company had enlisted for three years or for the war and on April 25, 1862, the men received their enlistment bounties.[27]

"Speights Regiment took up the line of march from Camp Crocket near Millican on the 29th June 1862"[28] for Arkansas, after a delay of three months caused by a shortage of transportation in the quartermaster department, a situation which bred bitter feelings and accusations of favoritism and personal gain before it was corrected. In easy stages the 15th Texas marched through Corsicana on July 20 to Camp Daniel in Smith County, where the regiment drilled and recruited from July 29 to September 9. Speight's command had then proceeded through Washington, Arkansas, on the 20th to Little Rock on October 5, leaving men behind in Texas to collect and forward clothing. Two weeks later on the 17th, the regiment had been among those sent to establish Camp Nelson in the wooded hill country east of Austin, Arkansas.

---

[26] Daniell, *Personnel of the Texas State Government*, 47-50; *Memorial and Biographical History of Dallas County, Texas*, 879-880; Warner, *Generals in Gray*, 126-127; *Biographical Encyclopedia of Texas* (New York, 1880), 174; Sidney Smith Johnson, *Texans Who Wore the Gray* (Tyler, 1907), 161-162; Lucy A. Erath, ed., *The Memoirs of Major George B. Erath, 1813-1891* (Waco, 1956), 94-97; Waco *Tribune-Herald*, October 30, 1949, July 19, 1953; L. E. Daniell, *Types of Successful Men of Texas* (Austin, 1890), 305-307; George Plunkett Red, *The Medicine Man in Texas* (Houston, 1930), 289-291; William M. Sleeper and Allan D. Sanford, *Waco Bar and Incidents of Waco History* (Waco, 1947), 169; Merle Mears Duncan, "David Richard Wallace, Pioneer in Psychiatry," *Texana*, I, 341-356; J. E. Harrison to Andrew Johnson, June 23, 1865, photocopy, Mrs. C. B. Tate Collection, Archives, University of Texas Library.

[27] Muster Rolls, Companies A, B, C, D, E, F, G, H, I, 15th Texas Infantry, Texas History Collection, Baylor University.

[28] James E. Harrison to [W. P. Ballinger], December 6, 1862, Ballinger Collection.

There the Texans suffered from dysentery and other camp diseases as did most new troops in the Civil War. Rumors of Union invasion efforts aimed at Texas, family problems at home, and fears about the outcome of the fighting in the Mississippi Valley intensified the gloom which often gripped members of the 15th Texas during the relatively inactive fall of 1862.

Brigadier General Henry E. McCulloch was ordered to organize the new units into an infantry division which he proceeded to do in October, 1862. The 15th Texas then found itself a part of McCulloch's 2nd Brigade, Colonel Horace Randal commanding. On November 23, the division marched for Camp Bayou Meto in the Arkansas River Valley where it was reviewed by the new department commander, Lieutenant General Theophilus Holmes.[29]

Early in December, 1862, "a shout throughout the camp" of the 15th Texas answered the receipt of march orders for Vicksburg, which had become the objective of Union forces advancing from Tennessee. After three days march through Little Rock to the east, however, the orders were countermanded. On December 14, new orders had started the disappointed regiment west to reinforce Hindman's army retreating from Prairie Grove. Speight's men met the retiring Confederate forces east of Van Buren on January 1, 1863, and fell back with Hindman to Clarksville. There the 15th Texas crossed the river at night in a cold rain without its baggage to assume a defensive position covering the town. Tensely the Texans awaited a Federal attack at dawn, but daylight came quietly and scouts later reported no enemy troops within eighty miles.

At nearby Piney Bayou on January 7, the "four demoralized Texas [dismounted cavalry] Regts were put under Col Speight"[30] creating the brigade with all of the basic units it would retain throughout the war, the 22nd Texas Dismounted Cavalry, the 31st Texas Dismounted Cavalry, the 34th Texas Dismounted Cavalry, and the 15th Texas Infantry, along with the 20th Texas Dismounted Cavalry. One of Speight's first acts was to dispatch officers to

---

[29] James E. Harrison to P. O. Hebert, April 30, 1862, to Dear Ballinger, July 11, December 5, 6, 1862, *ibid.*; P. O. Hebert to H. H. Sibley, August 8, 1862, *Official Records*, Series I, Vol. IX, 731; Special Orders No. 39, Hdqrs. Trans-Mississippi Department, September 28, 1862, *ibid.*, Series I, Vol. XIII, 884; Joseph P. Blessington, *The Campaigns of Walker's Texas Division* (New York, 1875), 43, 44, 61, 62, 64; J. B. Thompson to My Dear Ma and Pa, September 7, 1862, in *Chronicles of Smith County*, II, 16; T. J. Haynes to J. W. Speight, October 27, 1862, John R. King Collection, Archives, Texas State Library; Hamilton Diary, June 29 - November 25, 1862.

[30] *Ibid.*, December 11, 1862 - January 7, 1863; James E. Harrison to Dear Ballinger, February 19, 1863, Ballinger Collection.

Texas to collect and return to the ranks deserters from the cavalry regiments.[31]

At Piney Bayou, General Holmes met Hindman's army and on January 11 he ordered the Texas brigade through Fort Smith to reinforce Brigadier General William Steele, the new commander of the Indian Territory. Back trudged the Texans in varying degrees of cold winter rain and snow, short of wagons, across a country already stripped of forage for men and animals. Snow piled up eight to ten inches deep in places, and a hundred mules from the teams for the supply wagons and an artillery battery froze to death. Cattle and oxen were broken to harness to meet the emergency and to bring the guns and supplies through.[32]

Colonel Speight went ahead to meet General Steele as the brigade neared Fort Smith. In his absence on January 13, a band of Union guerrillas struck the Confederate supply train by surprise, disarmed its small guard detail, and captured much needed corn and some of the better wagon stock. Most of the corn was quickly recaptured, and Lieutenant Colonel Harrison of the 15th Texas pursued with ten mounted men and a company of infantry on January 14, covering over thirty miles through snow. He located the raiders but could not close with them because they were mounted. Texas cavalry under Lieutenant Colonel R. P. Crump solved that problem soon after their arrival next day by capturing the guerrillas including their captain, Martin D. Hart, a Unionist and former state senator from North Texas, who was hanged on January 20 for the brutal acts of his men against civilians in western Arkansas.[33]

In January, 1863, rumor also connected the 22nd and the 34th Texas with a secret Unionist organization which had been discovered in North Texas during the fall of 1862. Apparently no member of either unit was found to be directly implicated in the movement, but the rate of desertion in both regiments continued to be excessively high and their general attitude well into the

[31] Dallas *Herald,* January 28, 1863; George W. Guess to Mrs. Sarah H. Cockrell, January 17, 1863.

[32] *Ibid.;* Hamilton Diary, January 11, 1863; James E. Harrison to Dear Ballinger, February 19, 1863, Ballinger Collection.

[33] *Ibid.;* J. F. Crosby to R. C. Newton, January 14, 1863, *Official Records,* Series I, Vol. XXII, Pt. 2, 772; William Steele to John R. Baylor, January 18, 1863, *ibid.,* 774; George W. Guess to Mrs. Sarah H. Cockrell, January 17, 1863; Hamilton Diary, January 13-20, 1863; Wooten, *Comprehensive History of Texas, 1685-1897,* II, 638; William E. Sawyer, "Martin Hart, Civil War Guerrilla," *Texas Military History,* III, 146-153.

spring of 1863 remained "unreliable, and to some extent disloyal."[34]

Speight's brigade camped near Fort Smith on January 15 in terrible condition from the grueling march, reduced by desertion, sickness, and battle to 1,432 men. Because of poor roads, swollen streams, and a lack of equipment and forage to get them through, Steele held the half-starved, ill-clothed infantry a few days on the Arkansas River. For lack of subsistence to maintain the Texans he then ordered the nearly destitute regiments south to winter quarters at Doaksville, except for the 20th Texas which was retained at Fort Smith for garrison duty. At Fort Smith there also occurred a seemingly temporary change of command for the 31st Texas, when Colonel T. C. Hawpe left the regiment under Lieutenant Colonel George W. Guess while he returned to Dallas. The change proved to be permanent, however, for Hawpe never returnd to his command, apparently for business reasons.

No supplies were found at Johnson's Depot or elsewhere on the march south despite Steele's efforts to provide for the Texans. Speight thus was forced to continue on to the Red River with starvation a momentary possibility in the bleak Indian lands. Lieutenant Colonel Harrison pushed on ahead with only one blanket, despite a light case of flu, and sent back beeves and flour to relieve the dangerous situation. He found no corn for the teams, however, until he reached the Red River, and many animals died as a result. Snow began to fall on February 3 and continued on the 4th, forcing the brigade to plod homeward through a blanket of white eight or nine inches deep. A thaw set in finally on February 7, and the weary Texans struggled into camp on the 8th. Alfred T. Howell of the 34th Texas vividly recalled that they

> lived for three weeks on cold flour (parched corn, ground to meal) and water. No tents, no blankets, hardly anything to keep life and soul together. Many and many a night have I slept on the frozen ground with nothing around me but a blanket with a lump of ice for a pillow. By day, I limped along in my rundown boots, holes wearing into my feet. At night, my feet swelled and I could not stand. Men died every day. They laid themselves down. They would not move and they died. Men died on the wagons. From Fort Smith to the Mouth of the Kiamichi [River] where we camped, our trail

---

[34] E. Kirby Smith to T. H. Holmes, May 16, 1863, *Official Records*, Series I, Vol. XXII, Pt. 2, 839-840; William A. Phillips to Major General Curtis, January 19, 1863, *ibid.*, 62; Thomas Barrett, *The Great Hanging at Gainesville; Cooke County, Texas, A. D. 1862* (Gainesville, 1885; reprinted Austin, 1961); Sam Acheson and Julie Ann Hudson O'Connell, eds., "George Washington Diamond's Account of the Great Hanging at Gainesville, 1862," *Southwestern Historical Quarterly*, LXVI, 331-414; Frank H. Smyrl, Unionism, Abolitionism, and Vigilantism in Texas, 1856-1865 (Master's thesis, University of Texas, 1961), 124-133.

was a long graveyard. The bones of dead horses and mules, with destroyed and castaway wagons, would have made almost a turnpike.[35]

It had been a march capable of testing well disciplined troops, much less the already demoralized men of Speight's brigade. Doubtlessly they agreed with Lieutenant Colonel Harrison, that "We have been *litterally* [*sic*] *marched to death*. We have lost More Men than we should have (probably) lost in a dozen pitched Battles."[36]

---

[35] Alfred Thomas Howell to his brother, January 11, 1866, in William E. Sawyer and Neal A. Baker, Jr., eds., "A Texan in the Civil War," *Texas Military History*, II, 276; Wooten, *Comprehensive History of Texas, 1685-1897*, II, 638-639; William Steele to R. C. Newton, January 15, 1863, *Official Records*, Series I, Vol. XXII, Pt. 2, 773; J. F. Crosby to D. H. Cooper, January 27, 1863, *ibid.*, 777-778; Steele to John [W.] Speight, January 28, 1863, *ibid.*, 779; Steele to J. B. Magruder, March 23, 1863, *ibid.*, 805; report of Steele, February 15, 1864, *ibid.*, Series I, Vol. XXII, Pt. 1, 29-32; George W. Guess to Mrs. Sarah H. Cockrell, February 8, 1863; Hamilton Diary, January 22 - February 8, 1863; Dallas *Herald*, February 4, 1863; James E. Harrison to Dear Ballinger, February 19, 1863, Ballinger Collection.

[36] *Ibid.*

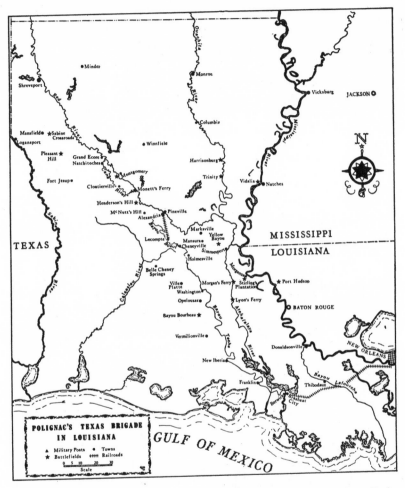

By Frances Parker

By Frances Parker

PRINCE CAMILLE DE POLIGNAC

BRIGADIER GENERAL JAMES E. HARRISON

COLONEL JOSEPH W. SPEIGHT

COLONEL ROBERT H. TAYLOR

BRIGADIER GENERAL WILBURN H. KING

COLONEL ALMERINE M. ALEXANDER

LIEUTENANT COLONEL GEORGE W. GUESS

LIEUTENANT COLONEL ASHLEY W. SPAIGHT

CHAPTER II

## *"Run right over them and give them Hell"*

## Louisiana, 1863

From Boggy Creek the brigade moved in mid-February to Camp Kiamichi near Doaksville in the Indian Territory just north of Clarksville, Texas. At that point Speight granted numerous furloughs to help restore morale and ordered all men absent from the brigade for any other reason to report immediately. Speight then returned to Waco for a short time, leaving the brigade under Colonel A. M. Alexander. Harrison also took leave of the brigade and returned to Arkansas in an effort to persuade General Holmes to send the 15th Texas to a combat area.[1] Without a definite answer Harrison returned to his regiment in late March. There, despite his personally apprehensive views of the war and of various morale problems at home, he began to drill the 15th Texas "three times a week in Battalion Drill and every day in Company drill,"[2] to ensure its readiness for active duty.

In the Indian Territory where the season for campaigning began early in the spring, Steele started to collect his army by ordering forward the Texas infantry brigade on March 20, 1863. Lacking confidence in the recently demoralized Texans, Steele counter-manded the order on March 31 and wrote Holmes in an attempt to replace them with more reliable troops. The Union Army refused to cooperate and Steele was forced to call for his infantry brigade again on April 9, because of a Federal troop concentration north and west of Fort Smith. Alexander delayed, however, apparently because Speight and many of the troops had not returned from leave. Impatient for reinforcements, Steele prodded Alexander on April 16 with orders to send the 15th Texas to Muddy Boggy Creek and to follow with the rest of the brigade as quickly as

---

[1] Dallas *Herald*, February 25, 1863; General Orders No. 16, Headquarters Speight's Brigade, February 20, 1863, Clarksville *Standard*, March 7, 1863; General Order No. 19, Headquarters 2nd (Speight's) Brigade, March 12, 1863, *ibid.*, March 14, 1863; Hamilton Diary, February 13-15, 1863; James E. Harrison to Dear Ballinger, March 23, 1862 [1863], Ballinger Collection.

[2] James E. Harrison to Dear Ballinger, March 31, 1863, *ibid.*

17

possible. Speight's regiment marched on April 21 and reached Johnson's Depot on the 27th. The dismounted cavalrymen prepared to follow them north with little joy at the prospect of continued service in the Indian Territory.[3]

At that moment in late April, 1863, Lieutenant General Edmund Kirby Smith, newly appointed commander of the Trans-Mississippi Department, changed the entire future of the Texas brigade by diverting its march to the army of Major General Richard Taylor at Alexandria, Louisiana. The Confederate forces in western Louisiana had just been driven from a position on Bayou Teche and were falling back before Major General Nathaniel P. Banks's superior Union army, which might be aiming at Shreveport, the location of department headquarters. Cavalry from Texas and Speight's infantry in the Indian Territory were the nearest units available to assist in halting the Federal advance.[4]

General Steele in the Indian Territory protested vigorously the loss of his infantry when he learned of the change in orders. His wrath reached a peak when he learned that Speight had taken Captain H. C. West's field battery to Louisiana as a part of the brigade. All efforts to have Speight arrested and the battery returned met with failure, however, because of Kirby Smith's priority decision in favor of Richard Taylor and the District of Western Louisiana.[5]

A brighter atmosphere prevailed almost immediately in the Texans' camp. By the first week in May the men of the 31st Texas were in "fine health and spirits and enjoy life hugely," noted Lieutenant Colonel Guess, although he hastened to add that "about two hundred [are] yet absent from the Reg'n and they are coming in rather slowly now."[6] To remedy the situation Guess and Alexander began to advertise for deserters and sent officers into home counties of the brigade's personnel to forward deserters to their regiments at Alexandria. The morale of the brigade received

[3] James E. Harrison to Dear Ballinger, April 21, 1863, *ibid.*; George W. Guess to Mrs. S. H. Cockrell, April 8, 1863; Hamilton Diary, April 21-27, 1863; William Steele to [A. M.] Alexander, March 20, 1863, *Official Records*, Series I, Vol. XXII, Pt. 2, 804-805; Steele to T. H. Holmes, March 31, 1863, *ibid.*, 809-810; Steele to Alexander, April 9, 16, 1863, *ibid.*, 815, 823.

[4] J. F. Belton to Commanding Officer Second Brigade Texas Volunteers, April 19, 1863, *ibid.*, Series I, Vol. XV, 1046; Richard Taylor, *Destruction and Reconstruction: Personal Experiences of the Late War* (New York, 1879; reprint ed. by Richard Harwell, New York, 1955), 153-154.

[5] William Steele to W. R. Boggs, May 14, June 8, 1863, *Official Records*, Series I, Vol. XXII, Pt. 2, 839, 862.

[6] George W. Guess to Mrs. S. H. Cockrell, May 5, 1863.

another blow on May 2, however, when Alexander's resignation because of continued ill health was accepted by Kirby Smith.[7]

The 15th Texas was ordered back to the Red River on April 29 and returned on May 6. The entire brigade then marched through Clarksville, Mount Pleasant, and Daingerfield to Jefferson on the 13th. There the Texans boarded steamers and arrived at Shreveport on May 14. Speight's brigade, variously estimated at 1,400 to 1,650 men, was thus concentrated for the use and inspection of the department commander. Kirby Smith was appalled at the sight of his much prized reinforcements, one-third of whom were unarmed. After a quick look at the brigade he felt that the 15th Texas Infantry and the 31st Texas Dismounted Cavalry were probably acceptable, but termed the other regiments, hardest hit by desertion, "an undisciplined mob; the officers as worthless as the men. . . ."[8] Incensed by the limited usefulness of the 22nd and the 34th Texas in that condition, Smith seriously considered placing the officers of both commands in the ranks and distributing the men among units of Major General John G. Walker's infantry division scheduled to arrive shortly thereafter at Shreveport. Instead, more sober second thoughts prevailed and the two regiments were placed in a camp of instruction to be disciplined and drilled as infantry.[9]

Speight, with the 15th Texas Infantry and the 31st Texas Dismounted Cavalry, was ordered on May 16 to Grand Ecore to reinforce Taylor. Arriving at that point on May 19 by steamer, the small command camped for a week, then continued down the Red River to Alexandria, which the Federals had evacuated only a few days earlier. From there Speight's brigade again boarded steamers on the 29th for Marksville, farther downstream. On May 30, the Texans marched to Simmesport where they camped for the next two weeks. During that period Speight's men skirmished with a Union gunboat and drove it off on June 3, only to be driven off in turn on June 4 by three Federal warships. The Texans were joined at that point by Taylor's Louisiana infantry

---

[7] Dallas *Herald,* May 13, 27, 1863; A. M. Alexander Carded File, War Department Collection of Confederate Records, National Archives. Deserters from the three dismounted cavalry regiments continued to come out of the East Texas brush throughout 1863. H. E. McCulloch to Edmund P. Turner, November 9, 1863, *Official Records,* Series I, Vol. XXVI, Pt. 2, 401.

[8] E. Kirby Smith to T. H. Holmes, May 16, 1863, *Official Records,* Series I, Vol. XXII, Pt. 2, 839-840.

[9] *Ibid.;* W. R. Boggs to Richard Taylor, May 14, 1863, *ibid.,* Series I, Vol. XV, 1083; Wooten, *Comprehensive History of Texas, 1685-1897,* II, 640; Hamilton Diary, April 29 - May 14, 1863.

brigade under Brigadier General Alfred Mouton on June 6, 1863.[10]

Speight then was ordered to Morgan's Ferry, twenty-five miles south. There the brigade crossed the Atchafalaya River and advanced to within five miles of the Mississippi River, hoping to reinforce or to assist in some way the garrison of Port Hudson then besieged by Banks's army. A crossing proved impossible and the Texans trudged back across the Atchafalaya. The infantrymen then marched south through Washington, Opelousas, New Iberia, and Franklin to rejoin Taylor's army as it began an offensive into the Bayou Lafourche region in an effort to relieve the pressure on Port Hudson. Speight's brigade crossed the Atchafalaya again on June 29 at Brashear City, just captured by Mouton's infantry and Brigadier General Thomas Green's cavalry, and pressed on to Thibodaux on July 1, 1863. There the Texas infantry rested until the 9th, covering Taylor's right flank while he planted batteries on the banks of the Mississippi to cut the Union supply line from New Orleans to Banks's army at Port Hudson.[11]

After Vicksburg and Port Hudson fell on July 4 and 9, Taylor concentrated his limited forces, including the Texas infantry, southwest of Donaldsonville to meet any Federal thrust across the Mississippi. Colonel Speight was placed under arrest at that time for what apparently proved to be only a difference of opinion with Colonel Joseph Bates, whose 13th Texas Infantry was temporarily attached to Taylor's army. As a result, Lieutenant Colonel James Harrison became acting brigade commander in time to lead the Texans on their march up Bayou Lefourche to Donaldsonville "with stagnant water on both sides and not a breath of air, no shade or place to rest" along the way.

Federal troops from Port Hudson, under Brigadier General Cuvier Grover, landed soon after Harrison's arrival. Taylor immediately prepared to fight a delaying action with his infantry and Green's cavalry. On July 13, 1863, at Kock's Plantation Harrison placed his infantry in an ambush position behind Green's cavalry who were expected to lead the Union advance into a trap. Instead, the impetuous Green led his dismounted troopers in a charge which routed the Federal force back into their earthworks on the banks of the Mississippi. The victory allowed time

---

[10] *Ibid.*, May 16 - June 14, 1863; Dallas *Herald*, June 3, 1863; Silas Grisamore, "Reminiscences," *Weekly Thibodaux Sentinel*, May 15, 1869; W. R. Boggs to J. W. Speight, May 16, 1863, *Official Records*, Series I, Vol. XXVI, Pt. 2, 6; E. Kirby Smith to Richard Taylor, May 16, 1863, *ibid.*, 7.

[11] R. Taylor to John L. Logan, June 15, 1863, *ibid.*, 53; George W. Guess to Mrs. S. H. Cockrell, July 6, 1863; A. C. Hill to T. M. Rector, July 28, 1863, Civil War Biographical File, Archives, University of Texas Library; Whetston Day Book, July 1, 1863.

for Taylor to remove captured stores from Brashear City. He then fell back across the Atchafalaya on July 18 to avoid being cut off and surrounded in the bayou country.[12]

Taylor's infantry force during the entire campaign had never exceeded 1,800 men in Speight's and Mouton's brigades. Because of his weakness in that arm and the availability of 5,000 rifles captured at Brashear City, Taylor had called on Kirby Smith in late June for the remainder of Speight's brigade.[13] Events had moved rapidly at Shreveport in the six week interval, however, and a new brigade was the immediate result. In their camp of instruction the two regiments left behind had been joined by elements of the Arkansas Post garrison who had escaped capture when the fort fell in January, 1863. The Arkansas Post men, representing seven regiments of infantry and dismounted cavalry, had been reorganized on July 1 as the 17th Texas Consolidated Dismounted Cavalry with youthful James R. Taylor, a former student at Larissa College in Texas, as colonel and Sebron M. Noble as lieutenant colonel. Under the direction of Colonel William H. Trader, a volunteer aide-de-camp to Kirby Smith, the discipline and instruction of the Texans as infantry had progressed well enough by the end of June for the three regiments to be organized into a brigade numbering 1,255 men present for duty.[14]

To command the new brigade Kirby Smith had a newly appointed brigadier general, Camille Armand Jules Marie, Prince de Polignac, son of the last prime minister of Charles X of France.

---

12 *Ibid.*, July 19, 1863; James E. Harrison to Dear Ballinger, August 8, 1863, Ballinger Collection; A. C. Hill to T. M. Rector, July 28, 1863, Civil War Biographical File; Estimate of troops in Trans-Mississippi Department after battle at Helena, *Official Records,* Series I, Vol. XXII, Pt. 1, 439.

13 R. Taylor to J. B. Magruder, July 17, 1863, *ibid.*, Series I, Vol. XXVI, Pt. 2, 116; report of Taylor, June 27, 1863, *ibid.*, Series I, Vol. XXVI, Pt. 1, 212.

14 E. W. H. Parker, "Seventeenth Texas Cavalry," in Johnson, *Texans Who Wore the Gray,* 302; D. S. Combs, "Texas Boys in the War," *Confederate Veteran,* XXXV, 265; Mamie Yeary, *Reminiscences of the Boys in Gray, 1861-1865* (Dallas, 1912), 34, 145, 674, 737; Wooten, *Comprehensive History of Texas, 1685-1897,* II, 640; Estimate of troops in Trans-Mississippi Department after battle at Helena, *Official Records,* Series I, Vol. XXII, Pt. 1, 439; General Orders No. 13, Headquarters Trans-Mississippi Department, May 23, 1863, *ibid.*, Series I, Vol. XXVI, Pt. 2, 16; Muster Roll, Company G, 34th Texas Dismounted Cavalry, June 30, 1863, photostat, Archives, University of Texas Library; George W. Guess to Mrs. S. H. Cockrell, September 9, 1863; Dallas *Herald,* June 17, 1863; List of Military Organizations Carded by the Record and Pension Office, Confederate, Texas Lists, 1-241, Record Group No. 94, National Archives, photostat, Texas State Library, 34; Rebecca W. Smith and Marion Mullins, eds., "The Diary of H. C. Medford, Confederate Soldier, 1864," *Southwestern Historical Quarterly,* XXXIV, 219. The Texas regiments captured at Arkansas Post were the 6th and the 10th infantry, and the 15th, 17th, 18th, 24th, and 25th dismounted cavalry.

He had served with the French army in the Crimean War and had been in Central America when the Civil War began. He had immediately offered his services to the Confederacy and had distinguished himself as a staff officer under Beauregard and Bragg east of the Mississippi. In appearance Polignac was "a typical Frenchman," thin and erect in stature with countenance which varied from grave to fiery according to the occasion, "a keen black eye, white teeth that showed brilliantly when he smiled," a Napoleon III beard, "and a dark waxed mustache which lent a fierceness to his expression. . . ."[15]

In reply to Taylor's June request for the Texas regiments, Smith sent word on July 12 that the new brigade was marching to Natchitoches where it was to be armed from Taylor's captures. Taylor then assumed the brigade to be a part of his command and ordered it farther south. But he soon learned that Polignac had taken command on the 20th and was digging entrenchments at Grand Ecore under direct orders from Smith, at the moment that Taylor's infantry were retreating across the Atchafalaya.[16]

Depressed in spirits by the fall of Vicksburg and Port Hudson, Taylor's army proceeded from the river up Bayou Teche on steamers through New Iberia to a camp outside Vermilionville where it remained until early September, 1863. At first the location was considered "very pleasant and rather a pretty camp," despite some outbreaks of sickness.[17] The health problem increased rapidly, however, until the nickname "Camp Dirreah [sic]"[18] seemed a more apt title for the spot and Lieutenant Colonel Guess complained "we are doing nothing here but getting sick and then trying to get well again."[19] Lieutenant Colonel Harrison, commanding the Texas brigade because of Speight's absence in

---

[15] Mrs. D. Giraud Wright, *A Southern Girl in '61; The War-Time Memories of a Confederate Senator's Daughter* (New York, 1905), 92; T. C. DeLeon, *Belles, Beaux and Brains of the 60's* (New York, 1909), 332; Count Michel de Pierredon, "Major General C. J. Polignac, C. S. A.," *Confederate Veteran*, XXII, 389; Warner, *Generals in Gray*, 241-242; Polignac to Beauregard, March 22, 1861, in *United Daughters of the Confederacy Magazine*, XXV, No. 10, p. 16; Harry J. Lemley, "General de Polignac," *ibid.*, XXVI, No. 1, p. 12; "Major General Prince de Polignac, C. S. A.," *ibid.*, XX, No. 1, pp. 14-15, 19, 22; Whetston Day Book, October 22, 1863.

[16] E. Kirby Smith to Richard Taylor, July 12, 1863, *Official Records*, Series I, Vol. XXVI, Pt. 2, 109; Taylor to E. Surget, July 14, 1863, *ibid.*, 111; W. R. Boggs to C. J. Polignac, July 16, 1863, *ibid.*, 113; Camille de Polignac Diary, July 20, 1863, microfilm, Russell Library, Northwestern State College of Louisiana.

[17] A. C. Hill to T. M. Rector, July 28, 1863, Civil War Biographical File.

[18] James E. Harrison to Dear Ballinger, August 8, 1863, Ballinger Collection; Whetston Day Book, August 8, 1863.

[19] George W. Guess to Mrs. S. H. Cockrell, August 22, 1863.

Texas for reasons of health, became increasingly worried as the sick list in his own regiment swelled to over a hundred and fifty. All the hospitals were full and many of the ill were forced to lie under trees "without a Blanket or some temporary covering and it rained almost every day for two weeks." Finally Harrison felt it necessary to send his son to Houston to acquire quinine for his prostrate command.[20]

While in camp at Vermilionville, Harrison also faced varying problems caused by changes in the composition of the brigade. First the remnants of Colonel Charles L. Pyron's 2nd Texas Mounted Rifles had been added to the brigade, dismounted, demoralized, and "deserting by the score at a time, stealing mules and horses"[21] in a mass effort to bypass orders and return to Texas. The situation, which was already extreme because the ranking officers of the unit were absent in Texas convalescing from wounds, grew steadily worse and Taylor soon ordered the few remaining members of the 2nd Texas to their home state.[22] On August 1, there also had been added to Speight's brigade the 218 men of Companies C, D, and E, 11th Texas Battalion, which had been recruited in the Beaumont area of East Texas. Lieutenant Colonel Ashley W. Spaight and Major Josephus S. Irvine, a veteran of the battle of San Jacinto, led the battalion into Louisiana in May, 1863. Since that time the men had fought at Brashear City and had been rearmed with Enfield and Springfield rifles from the ordnance stores taken there. Spaight's request on September 2, that his battalion be returned to Texas, was pocketed almost immediately since Taylor again was preparing for active campaigning.[23]

A Union division had been landed in early September at Morganza on the Mississippi near the mouth of the Red River. Taylor immediately sent most of his cavalry and infantry under Green to hold the line of the Atchafalaya against a possible Federal ad-

---

[20] J. E. Harrison to Captain Moncure, October 20, 1863, Guy M. Bryan Collection, Archives, University of Texas Library; Harrison to Dear Ballinger, August 31, 1863, Ballinger Collection.

[21] James E. Harrison to Dear Ballinger, August 8, 1863, ibid.; Whetston Day Book, August 17, 1863.

[22] R. Taylor to W. R. Boggs, September 2, 1863, Official Records, Series I, Vol. XXVI, Pt. 2, 199; Wooten, Comprehensive History of Texas, 1685-1897, II, 613.

[23] Ibid., 634; A. W. Spaight to J. B. Jones, September 2, 1863, Spaight Collection, Archives, University of Texas Library; J. S. Irvine to My Dear Wife, July 14, 1863, in possession of Jesse J. Lee, Houston, Texas; Cooper K. Ragan, Josephus Somerville Irvine, 1819-1876, The Worthy Citizen (Houston, 1963); Cooper K. Ragan, ed., "The Diary of Captain George W. O'Brien, 1863," Southwestern Historical Quarterly, LXVII, 30-31, 47-48.

vance toward Alexandria. Speight's brigade was held in readiness for a move through half the day on September 7 while arrangements were made to leave the more seriously ill behind for lack of transportation. Then the Texans marched fourteen miles to Carencro Bayou. On September 8, the march continued ten miles to a bayou below Opelousas, and word filtered down through the ranks that Green's cavalry were skirmishing along the Atchafalaya. The brigade covered twelve miles to reach Bayou Boeuf above Washington on the night of the 9th. From there the Texas infantry marched twenty-six miles to a camp near Morgan's Ferry on the Atchafalaya by September 11. Cavalry skirmishes continued along the river and an artillery duel accompanied by sniping took place on the 13th. After intermittent skirmishes a Federal advance was reported on September 17. Baggage, supplies, and sick were sent to the rear as the brigade formed a line of battle to defend its camp. Pickets again exchanged shots but that proved to be the extent of the day's action. Quiet then prevailed along the Atchafalaya until 10:00 A.M. on September 19 when the Texans received orders for a march that afternoon. At 1:00 P.M., Speight's brigade moved out to the west toward Washington, leaving additional sick behind in camp. The infantry regiments covered ten miles that afternoon and added twelve more on the morning of Sunday, September 20, with bursts of humor enlivening the march. When the drums sounded "Fall in" after lunch, however, the Texans were dismayed to find themselves marching back along the road over which they had just come. Early in the afternoon of the 21st the brigade reached its old camp on the Atchafalaya, but at three o'clock a warning sounded and the Texans formed for action. Skirmish fire increased across the river for half an hour then died out. The Confederate loss was one picket wounded. Speight's brigade remained in camp from the 22nd through the 27th, enjoying the cool, pleasant fall weather which had begun on September 19. It had been a trying period for the brigade filled with marching, confusion, and Speight's arrest of Lieutenant Colonel Guess on charges of trading with the enemy. On the positive side, the health of the Texas infantry had improved despite some rain and a steady diet of sweet potatoes.[24]

Late in the evening of Sunday, September 27, came word that Green planned to attack the Federal advance post at Stirling's Plantation on Bayou Fordoche. The Texans prepared two days

---

[24] *Ibid.*, 48-54; George W. Guess to Mrs. S. H. Cockrell, September 9, 15, 22, 1863, July 4, 1864; Hamilton Diary, September 7-21, 1863; Galveston *News*, May 19, 1865; Ludwell H. Johnson, *Red River Campaign: Politics and Cotton in the Civil War* (Baltimore, 1958), 64-65.

rations on the 28th and received march orders for 4:00 P.M. At that time most of Green's command began to cross the river on two flat ferry boats: first Waller's and Rountree's cavalry battalions, then Mouton's and Speight's infantry brigades, and finally Green's cavalry brigade which was across by one o'clock the next morning. One regiment from Colonel James P. Major's cavalry brigade already had been sent across the Atchafalaya at Lyon's Ferry to intercept any Federal reinforcements that might advance from Baton Rouge. The rest of Major's men remained west of the river to hold Morgan's Ferry. Green's plan of attack called for the infantry to march to the Union rear while the cavalry advanced to attack the Federal position from the front.[25]

Once the brigade had crossed the Atchafalaya about 7:00 P.M., Harrison moved his men three quarters of a mile downstream where they rested on their arms in drizzling rain through a sleepless night. At dawn on Tuesday, September 29, 1863, the infantry countermarched up river through a field of cockleburs, then away from the waterway along a swamp trail to the Morganza Road two miles behind the Federal camp. At approximately 1:00 P.M. Colonel Henry Gray, commanding both infantry brigades in Mouton's absence, placed the Louisiana brigade across the road to block the route of advance for any reinforcements from Morganza and to block the route of escape for any stragglers from the Federal command at Stirling's Plantation. Harrison then was ordered to move his brigade across a levee into a canefield and advance on the enemy. The 15th Texas under Major John W. Daniel led the column over the levee followed by the 31st Texas commanded by Major Frederick Malone, the 11th Texas Battalion under Lieutenant Colonel Spaight, and a Louisiana battalion commanded by Lieutenant Colonel F. H. Clack. In two files the long Confederate column continued a zig-zag course for over a mile until it came under fire from the sugar plantation buildings at a distance of about four hundred yards. Confusion ensued for a few minutes as each unit in turn moved to the right down rows of cane to form a line facing the Union position. By instinct more than command the Texans soon began a ragged advance toward the Federal fire. A short rush forward brought the 600 infantrymen to a ditch which provided them with cover. "The command of Fire was given, heard, and the entire line

25 Report of Thomas Green, October 2, 1863, *Official Records*, Series I, Vol. XXVI, Pt. 1, 329-332, also in Theophilus Noel, *A Campaign From Santa Fe to the Mississippi* . . . (Shreveport, 1865; reprint ed. by Martin H. Hall and Edwin A. Davis, Houston, 1961), 97-101; Ragan, ed., "The Diary of Captain George W. O'Brien, 1863," *Southwestern Historical Quarterly*, LXVII, 235-236.

discharged their pieces with very little, if any, effect" because the high cane hid the enemy lines.[26]

Harrison then ordered a charge on the Union held plantation, although as he described it:

> The advance upon his [the Federal] position was compelled to be through an open field; some four hundred yards through apalling [sic] fire from his Entire force. He Enfiladed me by occupying with a portion of his forces a large Sugar Mill and building connected with them. I detatched [sic] a portion of my command [Spaight's battalion] and dislodged them, and with the same detachment attacked his flank forcing him to abandon his first position and Change his front. I availed myself of this and charged him driving him into the Negro quarter, where we fought from house, to House, and street to street desperately. I discovered directly that a number of them were hiding in and under the Houses and Shooting my men from the rear, when I detatched [sic] a few men and ordered them to burst open the doors and clear out from in and under. Thus we passed through the Quarter, driving them before us until we drove them over a high livy [sic] which was his rear, and he changed his front to the rear and made a hard fight using two pieces of artilary [sic] all the time (Rifle Parrott). His last movement was to cover a flank movement on my left with his cannon, hiding his forces behind this high livy [sic], to a deep broad ditch running perpindicularly [sic] from the livy [sic] and commanding my flank. We were now fighting very close. I discovered his intention, met his flank movement driving them back and at the same time flanked him on the left, producing a rout of all of his left. At this time Maj [H. H.] Boone Came up from below and made a cavalry charge [with Waller's and Rountree's battalions] on his [the Federal] right producing an entire rout, but very few guns were fired by the Emey [sic] after Boone came in sight. Thy [sic] were whipped and running.[27]

Federal infantrymen began to throw down their arms in mass after an hour of heavy fighting, for Green's trap had closed neatly around them.

The Union command, which had consisted of 854 men from six units, had been completely surprised and routed as its casualties of sixteen killed, forty-four wounded, and 453 captured bore out in detail. Only the Federal cavalrymen had escaped in large numbers.[28] Casualties in Speight's brigade were heaviest in the

---

[26] *Ibid.*, 235-237; report of Thomas Green, October 2, 1863, *Official Records*, Series I, Vol. XXVI, Pt. 1, 329-332; A. W. Hyatt Diary, September 29, 1863, in Napier Bartlett, *Military Record of Louisiana; Including Biographical and Historical Papers Relating to the Military Organization of the State* (New Orleans, 1875), [Part 3], p. 11; W. R[andolph] H[owell] to Editor Telegraph, October 1, 1863, Houston *Tri-Weekly Telegraph*, October 9, 1863; J. S. Irvine to Dear Wife, October 3, 1863, in possession of Jesse J. Lee, Houston, Texas; Green to My Dear Wife, October 1, 1863, *Southern Historical Society Papers*, III, 62-63.

[27] [J. E. Harrison] to Dear Ballinger, October 8, 1863, Ballinger Collection.

[28] Report of N. J. T. Dana, September 30, 1863, *Official Records*, Series I, Vol. XXVI, Pt. 1, 321-322; Return of Casualties in the Union forces engaged at Stirling's Plantation, September 29, 1863, *ibid.*, 325; Nannie M. Tilley, ed., *Federals on the Frontier: The Diary of Benjamin F. McIntyre, 1862-1864* (Austin, 1963), 227-229; Richard B. Irwin, *History of the Nineteenth Army Corps* (New York, 1892), 273.

15th Texas which suffered fifteen killed, fifty-two wounded including Major Daniel, and one missing. The 31st Texas had had one killed, twelve wounded, and four missing. Lieutenant Colonel Guess, who had accompanied the regiment into action although under arrest, was captured while attending the wounded. In Spaight's battalion there were six dead, ten wounded, and three missing. The brigade total of 104 killed, wounded, and missing was unquestionable proof that Harrison's men had carried the battle for Green, since the total Confederate casualties numbered 121.[29] Green and Mouton in their reports gave special mention to the excellent leadership of Harrison, Spaight, and Daniel.[30]

After the battle, Harrison led his weary Texans back along the Morganza Road to Morgan's Ferry as a guard for Semmes' battery, which had bogged down in mud and had never reached the field. By the night of September 30, Speight's brigade was back in its camps west of the Atchafalaya resting from two days of marching and fighting in mud and almost continuous rain. Thursday, October 1, brought a clear cool end to the rain and the infantry recuperated in camp through October 4.[31]

With "Everyone in excellent spirits" the brigade marched fourteen miles west on the 5th. That evening word of nearby honey led members of Spaight's battalion into a swamp where they cut down a bee tree and enjoyed its delicacies until after dark. The Texans then moved to Moundville, three miles north of Washington, on the 6th as rumors began to spread through the ranks of a Federal advance up Bayou Teche toward Vermilionville and possibly Texas. A sixteen-mile march along the road to Alexandria on Wednesday, the 7th, brought the infantry out of the swamp country to Ville Platte on a rolling prairie dotted with groves of timber. Some of the Texans tried to buy chickens in the small town, only to meet with tales of suffering from Yankee occupation; but they were consoled with eggs, yams, rum, tobacco,

---

[29] Houston *Tri-Weekly Telegraph*, October 9, 1863; report of Thomas Green, October 2, 1863, *Official Records*, Series I, Vol. XXVI, Pt. 1, 332; [J. E. Harrison] to Dear Ballinger, October 8, 1863, Ballinger Collection; George W. Guess to Mrs. S. H. Cockrell, October 12, 1863. George W. O'Brien of Spaight's battalion estimated the brigade's loss at twenty-nine killed and seventy-four wounded. Ragan, ed., "The Diary of Captain George W. O'Brien, 1863," *Southwestern Historical Quarterly*, LXVII, 241. See also "Battle of Fordoche," in *The New Texas School Reader Designed For the Use of Schools in Texas* (Houston, 1864; reprinted Austin, 1962), 102-104; J. S. Irvine to Dear Wife, October 3, 1863, in possession of Jesse J. Lee, Houston, Texas; Hamilton Diary, September 28-29, 1863.

[30] Report of Thomas Green, October 2, 1863, *Official Records*, Series I, Vol. XXVI, Pt. 1, 331; report of Alfred Mouton, October 4, 1863, *ibid.*, 329.

[31] Ragan, ed., "The Diary of Captain George W. O'Brien, 1863," *Southwestern Historical Quarterly*, LXVII, 242-243, 413.

and a game of billiards. Early the next morning, the Texans were up marching west again but only for twelve miles on the 8th to Chicot, a town of "three buildings and . . . 4 hotel signs." On October 9, they continued on past Belle Cheney Springs, a prewar summer resort, to a camp in the piney woods two miles beyond. After a day's rest, Harrison led them back through town and north fourteen miles to Jackson's Bridge on the 11th while new rumors placed the Federals at Vermilion Bridge. On the 12th, the Texans again started north, then swung east through Cheneyville, an area of large sugar plantations, to a camp three miles below town as Taylor manuevered his limited forces before the Union thrust.[32]

Colonel Joseph Speight arrived from Texas on October 13, resumed command of the brigade, and led it south eight miles along Bayou Boeuf during an afternoon filled with rumors of 25,000 Yankees under Major General William B. Franklin below at Carencro Bayou. Taylor's entire army was concentrating, and the Texas regiments of Walker's division and the Louisiana units of Mouton's brigade again were nearby. Speight's men marched through Holmesville and continued south for twelve miles on the 14th before camping in a pasture. During the day Lieutenant Colonel Spaight had rejoined his command from Alexandria, where he again had tried in vain to have his battalion returned to Texas. On the 15th, the Texans covered seventeen miles and camped near Moundville soon after lunch. At 7:00 P.M., with rumors abounding, the infantrymen received orders to cook two days' rations. A fight seemed imminent. March orders were issued, then countermanded, and Taylor's infantry brigades rested in camp from the 16th until the 21st, with "Preaching three times during the day but no obdurate sinners converted" on Saturday and Sunday, the 17th and 18th, and a revival promised for the near future.[33]

While Speight's brigade had marched and fought in southern Louisiana during the fall of 1863, Polignac's brigade had been held in reserve near Alexandria. There its new commander had made continued efforts to settle lingering discipline and morale problems, which reached a peak in early September with numerous desertions from the 22nd and the 34th Texas. In that same period, John H. Caudle, an experienced soldier, had been placed in command of the 34th Texas and promoted to lieutenant colonel, following the resignation of the regiment's field officers, while

---

[32] *Ibid.*, 413-417; Hamilton Diary, October 5-12, 1863.

[33] *Ibid.*, October 13-15, 1863; Ragan, ed., "The Diary of Captain George W. O'Brien, 1863," *Southwestern Historical Quarterly*, LXVII, 417-422.

Robert D. Stone had become colonel of the 22nd Texas in place of Stevens who had resigned for lack of ability to control his men. Conditions had improved, however, and on October 18 Polignac's command joined Taylor's army. It was merged immediately with Speight's command to form a consolidated brigade composed of the 15th Texas Infantry, the 22nd Texas Dismounted Cavalry, the 31st Texas Dismounted Cavalry, the 34th Texas Dismounted Cavalry, the 17th Texas Consolidated Dismounted Cavalry, and the 11th Texas Battalion. Polignac received command of the brigade by virtue of his rank and Speight again returned home, primarily because of his continued ill health. The Texans at first were wary of the dapper Frenchman with the unpronounceable name and some threatened not to serve under him. Taylor reminded the men of their duty, then promised to remove Polignac if they remained unhappy with him after he had led them in action. Tension eased thereafter, especially once the Texans dubbed their new commander "Polecat" in a caricature of his name.[34]

Immediately after the change in command, Harrison outlined to Polignac the causes for a degree of demoralization in the brigade: absence, lack of energy, and failure to enforce discipline and to set an example for the men on the part of the regimental officers; excessive non-combat details; sickness; and a lack of certain provisions—especially shoes and clothing. But the Texan closed on the hopeful note that both health and discipline were much improved.[35]

Cavalry skirmishes and artillery cannonades had continued at the front below Opelousas while the infantry drilled, rested, and

[34] *Ibid.*, 420-421; J. E. Harrison to My Dear Son, October 18, 1863, Harrison Papers, Texas History Collection, Baylor University; A. C. Hill to [T. M. Rector?] November 6, 1863, Civil War Biographical File; Whetston Day Book, October 26, 1863; Elijah P. Petty to Frank Petty, September 5, 1863, Petty Papers, Mansfield Battle Park Museum, Mansfield, Louisiana; Dave to Dear Mother, September 11, [1863], David M. Ray Collection, Archives, University of Texas Library; Polignac Diary, August-September, 1863; Taylor, *Destruction and Reconstruction*, 183-184; Wright, *A Southern Girl in '61*, pp. 92-93; James G. Stevens Carded File, War Department Collection of Confederate Records, National Archives; John H. Caudle Carded File, *ibid.* Colonel Speight was recommended for promotion by Kirby Smith in November, 1863, but he resigned in the spring of 1864, apparently having never returned to active duty. Later there were rumors about possible misbehavior in battle, but ill health would appear to have been the basic cause for his resignation. Report of E. Kirby Smith, November 8, 1863, *Official Records*, Series I, Vol. XXVI, Pt. 1, 385; J. W. Speight to J. E. Harrison, December 6, 1863, photocopy, Tate Collection; Special Orders No. 92, Hdqrs., Trans-Mississippi Department, April 15, 1864, War Department Collection of Confederate Records, National Archives; Merle Mears Duncan, ed., "An 1864 Letter to Mrs. Rufus C. Burleson," *Southwestern Historical Quarterly*, LXIV, 371.

[35] J. E. Harrison to Captain Moncure, October 20, 1863, Bryan Collection.

ate sugar cane. On October 21, the skirmishing drew nearer and at 10:00 A.M. Polignac's men received an order to prepare to march. Wagons were loaded and the Texas infantry proceeded twelve miles up the Boeuf by dark. In a rain which lasted two days the Texans moved their camp two miles into a wooded area and built fires in an attempt to dry themselves. The 22nd and the 34th Texas moved to the front on October 24 to support Green's cavalry but saw no action. In the camp men of Spaight's battalion varied their diet with pumpkins silently requisitioned from a nearby field. On the 25th, the brigade marched fourteen miles to a camp in a briar patch near Holmesville, then on to Cheneyville on October 26. There Polignac's brigade remained until November 8, its rest interrupted only by rain, a drinking spree on the 30th in Company C of Spaight's battalion and in Company D of the 22nd Texas, the beginning of a religious revival, and the departure of the 15th Texas.[36]

Harrison's regiment was separated from the brigade on October 29 by orders to report to Green for picket duty eighteen miles below Moundville. The Texans marched south in a drenching rain and pressed on to Washington by November 2 under additional orders. There they were joined by the 18th Texas Infantry, commanded by Colonel Wilburn Hill King, which had been detached from Walker's division for similar duty. About two o'clock on the morning of November 3, both regiments were ordered to Opelousas where they were joined at daybreak by the 11th Texas Infantry commanded by Colonel Oran M. Roberts. Breakfast was hurriedly eaten during an hour's rest, then Green moved south with the cavalry brigades of Major and A. P. Bagby and the three infantry regiments under Roberts, the senior colonel. Three miles from the camp of Brigadier General S. G. Burbridge's Federal brigade on Bayou Bourbeau, Green halted his troops to organize a plan of attack. Major's brigade was to advance mounted over an open prairie to the west and strike the Union left flank; Bagby's men were to move forward dismounted directly west of the road; while Roberts' infantry were to charge south through a partially timbered area between bayou and road. Roberts aligned his men with the 11th Texas, 355 strong, on the left; the 18th Texas, 320 men, in the center; and the 15th Texas, 275 strong, on the right because its members had longer range Enfield Rifles and would be more exposed in the advance. Two companies of the 15th Texas and one from the 11th Texas were thrown out

---

[36] Ragan, ed., "The Diary of Captain George W. O'Brien, 1863," *Southwestern Historical Quarterly*, LXVII, 421-424; A. C. Hill to [T. M. Rector?] November 6, 1863, Civil War Biographical File; Hamilton Diary, October 21-26, 1863.

as skirmishers. Green rode by and called for Harrison to "run right over them and give them Hell," which he passed on to his men who replied "right Col[onel]."[37]

Then came the order to advance, and, in Harrison's words,

The command moved by the right flank, Skirmishers thrown out. Directly the "Ball was fairly opened." I brought my command in to line rapidly to support the Skirmishers, . . . first by companies into line then forward into line, by companies left half wheel. *Double Quick*, without halting we were in line and on we went. Now the Eney [sic] Cannon being in good Range opened on me. The other Regts came into line in the Timber on my left. And the fight commenced in good earnest and on we went, over deep Gullies, on the right Ravines and points of Timber. Thus my course led, and My Command was much exposed all the time to the Enemie [sic] Battery and a concentrated fire from his Enfields and Musketry. My command was in plain view of them. We drove them Back one mile and a half to their main encampment before which was a deep ravine. This was exactly to my front, and here thy [sic] made a desperate stand, and I too, for the first time was in the timber. It seemed to rain Minee [sic] Balls, grape and sheel [sic]. With out Counting noses, I sprang before my men and ordered a charge. A Shout and a rush then our Rifles told on their routed fleeing confused masses, and thy [sic] ley [sic] in heeps [sic]. About this time Adjutant [John B.] Jones Informed me that we had been flanked by a regt of the Enemee [sic] Cavaly [sic] and they were about to charge us from the rear, when I faced my command by the Rear Rank and Charged them, producing among them before my line a scene of wild confution [sic], Men tumbling from Horses, screaming, Others throwing up their hands for mercy, Horses running wildly over the field without riders, others rooling [sic] and tumbling. Directly all was still. We pursued in the direction of the fleeing Eney [sic] across the bayou through the timber where Genl Green had a Battery brought forward and our three Regts drawn up to protect it. Then an artilly [sic] duel took place, the shell falling thick around us, . . . The Enemy having received heavy reinforcements [Weitzel's division, 19th Corps], after remaining in position half [an] hour, Genl Green ordered us to retire placing a cavaly [sic] command in our rear. We had gone about three fourths of a mile when skirmishing was heard to the rear, And directly Green's Cavaly [sic] Came dashing along in wild confusion. He could not rally them. Genl Green sent an aid to me to bring back my Regt. to cover his troops . . . . Without halting I gave the command counter march by the left flank by files right double quick march. My jaded and Battle worn men responded, gloriously and in the presence of Genl Green we came into line in the open prairy [sic] behind a hedge and before the Enemy. They saw me in line and did not give us Battle. I remained in This position until Genl Green ordered me to move my command one 3/4's of a mile to the rear of the other troops to camps which I did without any thing occuring [sic].[38]

---

[37] *Ibid.*, October 30 - November 3, 1863; James E. Harrison to Dear Ballinger, November 9, 1863, Ballinger Collection; O. M. Roberts to E. R. Wells, November 6, 1863. Roberts Collection, Archives, University of Texas Library; E. R. Wells to Officer Commanding Infantry at Washington Bridge, November 2, 1863, *ibid.*; Blessington, *Walker's Texas Division*, 138-139; report of Thomas Green, November 4, 1863, *Official Records*, Series I, Vol. XXVI, Pt. 1, 393-395, also in Noel, *A Campaign From Santa Fe to the Mississippi*, 104-106.

[38] James E. Harrison to Dear Ballinger, November 9, 1863, Ballinger Collection.

Accompanying the "dirty and ragged" Texans as they fell back to Opelousas after the victory were great numbers of Federal prisoners, most of whom were from Burbridge's brigade of the 13th Corps. Union losses totaled twenty-five killed, 129 wounded, and 562 missing, mostly in Confederate hands. Also captured were three field guns although only one could be removed from the field.[39]

Infantry had again carried the brunt of the battle for Green as Southern losses testified. Out of a total loss of 182 killed, wounded, and missing, Roberts' regiments had suffered 141 casualties. The 15th Texas had lost nine killed, twenty-one wounded including Captain Richard Coke, and three missing.[40] On November 4, Confederate details buried the dead left on the battlefield and collected their wounded in the courthouse at Opelousas where sympathetic women of the area cared for them. Roberts' three regiments then marched back to the field of action to camp on the 7th, the Federal forces having retired through New Iberia toward Berwick Bay.[41]

Roberts moved his Texans again on November 20 under orders from Green to join Taylor's infantry brigades at Simmesport where they had marched between the 9th and 11th. The Texas and Louisiana infantry had then crossed the Atchafalaya to support Confederate field batteries shelling Union transports on the Mississippi. While the men of the 15th Texas plodded after their brigade, Spaight's battalion, the 22nd, and the 31st Texas picketed the Mississippi River bank at Hogs Point with "no fire, drizzling rain, a Norther and an insufficiency of rations," on the 19th. They were again on picket duty on November 24 as Harrison's men approached east of the Atchafalaya. Skirmishing continued along

---

[39] *Ibid.;* J. T. Woods, *Services of the Ninety-Sixth Ohio Volunteers* (Toledo, 1874), 43-49; Irwin, *Nineteenth Army Corps,* 277-278; Return of Casualties in the Union forces engaged at Bayou Bourbeau, November 3, 1863, *Official Records,* Series I, Vol. XXVI, Pt. 1, 359; report of Thomas Green, November 4, 1863, *ibid.,* 393-395.

[40] *Ibid.;* O. M. Roberts to E. R. Wells, November 6, 1863, Roberts Collection; James E. Harrison to Dear Ballinger, November 9, 1863, Ballinger Collection; Blessington, *Walker's Texas Division,* 142, 144; List of Casualties . . . in the 15th (Speight's Regiment) T. V. I. at the Battle of Borbeux, November 3, 1863, Exum to Ed. Telegraph, November 6, 1863, Houston *Tri-Weekly Telegraph,* November 16, 1863; List of Casualties . . . in battle of Bayou Bourbeau, November 3, 1863, *ibid.,* November 20, 1863; Hamilton Diary, November 3, 1863.

[41] *Ibid.,* November 7, 1863; Blessington, *Walker's Texas Division,* 145; James E. Harrison to Dear Ballinger, November 16, 1863, Ballinger Collection; E. R. Wells to O. M. Roberts, November 10, 1863, Roberts Collection.

the river while the units in camp drilled in cool fall weather as November came to an end.[42]

Polignac's reunited brigade marched twenty miles south on December 1, returned to camp by the 3rd, then rushed off across the Fordoche without breakfast. On the 5th the Texans returned to camp on the site of their earlier victory, Stirling's Plantation. A move toward Morganza on the 7th was followed by picket duty on the 9th. The Texas infantry recrossed the Atchafalaya on December 10 and Lieutenant Colonel Spaight left to see Taylor in a third effort to get his battalion sent to Texas. In his absence the brigade marched up river to Bayou de Glaize on the 12th and to Mansura on the 14th. Some of the troops acquired liquor in the small village and made the "night hideous with Bacchanalian songs, yells and oaths emanating principally from Stephens' [sic] and Alexander's Regts." The Texans continued toward Alexandria the next day over terrible roads with numerous tipsy stragglers and camped about 10:00 P.M. in a rain which lasted until morning.

An effort was made to cross the Red River on December 16 but only the 17th Texas reached the north bank. The other units floundered through the mud back to their camps with wet equipment and bedding to spend a miserably cold night.[43] Polignac and his staff, however, found two surgeons of Mouton's brigade high and dry at a house in Mansura and proceeded to join them. An informal party ensued and "the gallant little French General, who was soon sufficiently mellow to be entertaining, . . . enlivened the house by singing every few minutes a verse of a song, which had reference to one 'Madam Gregoire' whoever she may have been," for egg nog "brought out the musical abilities and loquacious qualities of the company."[44]

A successful crossing was made on December 17 with the 34th Texas leading, followed by the 22nd and the 31st Texas, Spaight's battalion, and the 15th Texas. The brigade then marched to within two miles of Alexandria on the 18th and 19th. There on

---

[42] Thomas Green to O. M. Roberts, November 19, 1863, *ibid.*; J. G. Walker to Roberts, November 24, 1863, *ibid.*; Hamilton Diary, November 20-30, 1863; Ragan, ed., "The Diary of Captain George W. O'Brien, 1863," *Southwestern Historical Quarterly,* LXVII, 425-428; J. E. Harrison to My Dear Son, December 11, 1863, Harrison Papers.

[43] *Ibid.*; Hamilton Diary, December 1-15, 1863; J. S. Irvine to My Dear Wife, December 10, 1863, in possession of Jesse J. Lee, Houston, Texas; Record Book, J. A. Buck's Company [F], Stevens' [22nd Texas Cavalry] Regiment, December 10-16, 1863, photostat, Archives, University of Texas Library, original in possession of Llewellyn Notley, Teague, Texas; Ragan, ed., "The Diary of Captain George W. O'Brien, 1863," *Southwestern Historical Quarterly,* LXVII, 428-431.

[44] Grisamore, "Reminiscences," *Weekly Thibodaux Sentinel,* July 17, 1869.

the 20th, Spaight's men learned of their commander's final success in having his battalion returned to Texas when they were put aboard the train for Lecompte. Taylor sent them off with a recommendation that Spaight be promoted to colonel and that the battalion be increased to a regiment; far better proof of their service in Louisiana than any words of praise.[45]

[45] Ragan, ed., "The Diary of Captain George W. O'Brien, 1863," *Southwestern Historical Quarterly*, LXVII, 431-432; R. Taylor to J. B. Magruder, December 19, 1863, Spaight Collection; Special Orders No. 328, Headquarters District of Western Louisiana, December 20, 1863, *Official Records*, Series I, Vol. XXVI, Pt. 2, 518.

Chapter III

# "My boys, follow your Polignac"

## Louisiana and Arkansas, 1864

As Spaight's men crossed the Red River and moved south on December 20, Polignac's brigade again shouldered arms and proceeded north toward Monroe in northeastern Louisiana. Over fifty miles of marching took the Texans through Winnfield on the 23rd, and sixty more brought them into camp two miles west of Monroe on the 26th. After two days in camp the brigade crossed the Ouachita River at Trenton and went into camp in the slave quarters on the Richardson Plantation east of Monroe on January 1, 1864. The weather turned freezing cold for a time, followed by rain, and some men became ill with pneumonia. On the 3rd, Polignac again moved his camp, this time south of Monroe where shoes were issued to the needy on the 5th. Little more happened until January 17 and 18 when the brigade began a march down the Ouachita River. Thirty-two uneventful miles brought the Texans to Columbia on the 19th. There they crossed the river on the 20th and continued south to Harrisonburg on January 24. The purpose of their march became clear at that point; they were to act as a covering force for Confederate engineers rebuilding the batteries on the river at Harrisonburg and at Trinity. Yet only drill in camp broke the monotony of life in "a poor miserable hilly pine woods country on our side [of the river], and swamps on the other, . . . no provissions [sic] or forage, all must be brought from other points."[1]

In early February, 1864, Polignac proposed a raid against lightly held Vidalia on the Mississippi River across from Natchez. Taylor approved the effort as a means of collecting horses and mules, clearing the area of jayhawkers and Union cotton planters, and capturing or at least providing an opportunity for desertion from the predominantly Negro garrison at Vidalia. Five hundred and

---

[1] J. E. Harrison to My Dear Son, February 2, January 1, 2, 4, 12, 1864, Harrison Papers; Harrison to Dear Ballinger, January 3, 1863 [1864], Ballinger Collection; Hamilton Diary, December 23, 1863 - January 24, 1864; Record Book, Company F, 22nd Texas, December 20, 1863 - January 30, 1864; A. H. May to A. Mouton, January 25, 1864, Official Records, Series I, Vol. XXXIV, Pt. 2, 914.

fifty men from the dismounted cavalry regiments crossed the Ouachita at 2:00 A.M. on February 6, and moved across the Tensas River before dark.

On February 7, the brigade marched down Concordia Lake and between two and three o'clock in the afternoon formed in a belt of timber separated from Vidalia by an open area two miles wide. Cotton bales blocking the streets warned the Texans that the element of surprise had eluded them. Polignac quickly decided to bluff an attack rather than retreat, hoping to gain time for his foragers who were rounding up live stock along the Mississippi. He sent three cavalry companies to cover the left fork of the road into the village and extended his infantry across to the right fork which also led into town. Skirmishers trotted out of the trees as Polignac rode to the front of his command. Rising in his stirrups the little Frenchman brandished his sword and called to the lean veterans "Follow me! Follow me! You call me 'Polecat,' I will show you whether I am 'Polecat' or 'Polignac!' "[2] The Texans went forward in a double line with three battle flags snapping and rifles at the "carry."

Forewarned, the Federal commander at Vidalia had sounded the alarm and reinforcements were rushed across from Natchez at 2:30 P.M. Three Union gunboats and an armed tug began to shell the advancing Confederates from the river. The Texans fell back to the woods in some confusion, but reorganized and came on again on the right, driving in Union pickets until the Confederate skirmishers were within a hundred yards of the Federal works, closely followed by the main battle line. Suddenly Union infantry arose from their protected position to deliver a volley at close range. The Texans threw themselves prone to escape the withering blast, took a second volley in that position, then withdrew to the timber. Federal gunboats and entrenched infantry were a rugged combination, hoped-for assistance east of the Mississippi had not appeared, and Polignac had no desire to waste men in useless assaults. Alfred T. Howell, adjutant of the 22nd Texas, interjected a note of levity into the scene of disappointment when "my horse ran away with me in the direction of the Federal lines.

---

[2] Wright, *A Southern Girl in '61*, pp. 92-93, does not specify the occasion on which this statement was made, but says the Texans "never had a word of ridicule more for Polignac." Comte de Paris, *History of the Civil War in America* (4 vols.; Philadelphia, 1875-1888), IV, 502-503, points out that Vidalia provided Polignac with the first opportunity to prove himself to the Texans. Taylor, *Destruction and Reconstruction*, 184, indicates Harrisonburg on March 2 as the occasion when Polignac won the respect of his men. But Taylor was not present, and that action, fought from behind levees against gunboats, provided no opportunity for such a scene.

I turned him, however, before he got very far, and as I came back, our men shouted that my horse was a Yankee."[3]

By nightfall the brigade had retired nine miles. Polignac led his men back to the Tensas on the 8th and into their camps at Harrisonburg by the 10th with almost four hundred cattle, horses, and mules, and a new respect for their commander. Brigade losses were six killed, ten wounded, and eight captured.[4]

Throughout the rest of February the Texas brigade remained relatively inactive at Harrisonburg and at Trinity where the engineers finally had decided to mount three thirty-two pounder cannon. For the last two weeks in February details of Polignac's men worked on the fortifications that would house the artillery. The earthworks were nearing completion but only one big gun was mounted, with no ammunition available, on the afternoon of March 1 when pickets down river reported the approach of six Federal gunboats. Engineers rolled two of the heavy cannon into shallow water near the river bank and buried a third in the fort before the Union warships appeared. After shelling the town from anchor for an hour, the gunboats moved on toward Harrisonburg just before dark. Polignac withdrew the 15th, the 31st, and the 34th Texas from Trinity across a pontoon bridge over Little River to concentrate his command, then hurried them on to Harrisonburg which he occupied with the 17th and the 22nd Texas.

Two gunboats appeared at 10:00 A.M. on March 2 to shell Harrisonburg, but the Texas infantry and a field battery hugged the river bank and held the town despite a heavy bombardment while damaging one Union vessel, the *Fort Hindman*. Once the warships had passed up river, Polignac withdrew his men to their camps a mile from town. It proved to be a somewhat hasty move for the gunboats returned an hour later, and Union sailors set fire to some buildings in the town before being driven out by the 31st Texas. The Texans then put out the fires and saved all but three houses under a steady cannonade from the warships. On March 3, the Federal gunboats moved back downstream to Trinity where they destroyed the pontoon bridge across Little River,

---

[3] Alfred Thomas Howell to his brother, January 11, 1866, in Sawyer and Baker, eds., "A Texan in the Civil War," *Texas Military History*, II, 278.

[4] A. H. May to C. J. Polignac, February 1, 1864, *Official Records*, Series I, Vol. XXXIV, Pt. 2, 934-935; C. Le D. Elgee to Polignac, February 8, 1864, *ibid.*, 952-953; report of Hubert A. McCaleb, February 9, 1864, *ibid.*, Series I, Vol. XXXIV, Pt. 1, 129-130; "Fight at Vidalia, La.," in Frank Moore, ed., *The Rebellion Record: A Diary of American Events . . .* (12 vols.; New York, 1861-1868), VIII, 377-378; report of James A. Greer, February 6-8, 1864, *Official Records of the Union and Confederate Navies in the War of the Rebellion* (31 vols.; Washington, 1894-1927), Series I, Vol. XXV, 737; Whetston Day Book, February 7-9, 1864; Polignac Diary, February 6-7, 1864; Record Book, Company F, 22nd Texas, February, 1864.

located the hidden artillery, and took the cannon with them as they steamed on toward the Red River. Confederate casualties totaled six killed and ten wounded, as compared to two killed and twelve wounded aboard the Union fleet. Loss of the big guns made the expedition a Confederate defeat of sorts. But rain had made the roads nearly impassable for infantry; removal of the heavy guns had been virtually impossible under the prevailing conditions. Again the Texas brigade had proved it could operate effectively under its new commander and had also cleared away most lingering doubts about the fighting qualities of the retrained dismounted cavalry regiments.[5]

Polignac reoccupied Trinity on March 8, but immediately thereafter received orders to join Taylor at Alexandria in expectation of a Federal advance under Banks up the Red River. On the 9th, the troops at Trinity were recalled and on the 10th the entire brigade filed out of Harrisonburg to the west. Steady marching brought the Texans to Pineville on the 14th, a day later than Taylor expected. Gray's brigade, formerly Mouton's, also had arrived at Alexandria; therefore the two brigades were ordered east through Lecompte on the 15th to reinforce Walker's division already skirmishing near Cheneyville. From Lecompte Taylor began his retreat into western Louisiana on March 16 with a twelve mile march toward Fort Jesup. Hard marching continued as the order of the day on the 17th and 18th when the Texas and Louisiana brigades reached Carroll Jones's, a Confederate supply depot in the piney woods where they were joined by Walker's division. There Polignac's and Gray's brigades were formally organized into an infantry division commanded by Brigadier General Mouton. On the 22nd, the Texas brigade was formed in line of battle for a time, probably because of the Federal surprise and capture of the Southern rear guard at Henderson's Hill the night before. A further move to Beasley's nearer Natchitoches was carried out on March 23 and the 22nd Texas camped near the Cane River on the 24th. After three days there the regiment rejoined the brigade, which marched north through Fort Jesup on March 30. By April 1, Polignac's men were only six miles from Pleasant Hill, where they were halted on the 2nd to form a line of battle on the Natchitoches road. The Texans marched north again on the 3rd and camped ten miles south of Mansfield. On the 4th, they passed through the small

---

[5] *Ibid.*, March 1-2, 1864; W. D. Flynn to Misses Cockrell, March 6, 1864; reports of Camille J. Polignac, March 3, 4, 1864, *Official Records*, Series I, Vol. XXXIV, Pt. 1, 155-158; report of F. M. Ramsey, March 5, 1864, *Official Records, Navies*, Series I, Vol. XXV, 787-789. See [St. John R.] Liddell, "Trans-Mississippi and Spanish Fort," *Southern Bivouac* (New Series), II, 737-738, for criticism of Polignac's efforts at Harrisonburg and Trinity.

town and camped alongside the Shreveport road, while Lieutenant Colonel James Harrison, on leave in Texas, bemoaned fate that let his horse run away and leave him afoot at such a time. In its camps north of Mansfield the Texas brigade rested through the 7th, while Green's cavalry skirmished with the Federal advance near Pleasant Hill.[6]

Polignac's brigade received new marching orders on the morning of April 8 and led Taylor's 5,300 infantry back through Mansfield to a pre-selected position three miles south at Sabine Crossroads. There Taylor placed Mouton's division to the left of the road and Walker's to the right on the fringe of a timbered area facing south across an open field. Polignac's brigade formed Mouton's right, while Gray's Louisiana brigade extended the line to the left and connected with Major's cavalry division covering the exposed left flank.[7]

Cavalry skirmishing continued throughout the day, but the Federals seemed suddenly timid after their prolonged advance up the Red River Valley and refused to attack. The Louisiana brigade on the Texans' left was especially anxious to fight the invaders of their state, and Mouton turned to Polignac at one point in the afternoon exclaiming "Let us charge them right in the face, and throw them into the valley."[8] Taylor, equally impatient, rode down the line about 4:00 P.M. and called out "Little Frenchman, I am going to fight Banks here, if he has a million men!" then ordered Mouton's division to charge.[9]

Both brigades rushed forward to a fence south of the field, paused, then swept on into the woods with a rebel yell. Union volleys staggered the Confederate advance and Mouton went down while leading his men into action. Killed also by the opening Federal fire was Lieutenant Colonel Sebron M. Noble of the 17th Texas Consolidated. Polignac immediately assumed command of

---

[6] Record Book, Company F, 22nd Texas, March 7 - April 7, 1864; Hamilton Diary, March 10 - April 4, 1864; James E. Harrison to My Dear Daughter, April 4, 1864, Ballinger Collection; A. H. May to C. J. Polignac, March 7, 1864, *Official Records*, Series I, Vol. XXXIV, Pt. 1, 573-574; R. Taylor to Major General Walker, March 15, 1864, *ibid.*, 578; Taylor to W. R. Boggs, March 15, 1864, *ibid.*, 495-496; Taylor, *Destruction and Reconstruction*, 185-190.

[7] *Ibid.*, 194-195; Polignac Diary, April 8, 1864; report of Richard Taylor, April 18, 1864, *Official Records*, Series I, Vol. XXXIV, Pt. 1, 563; J. E. Hewitt, *1864 Battle of Mansfield, Mansfield, Louisiana* (Mansfield, 1925; reprinted, Mansfield, 1949), 2; Alonzo H. Plummer, *Battle of Mansfield or Sabine Cross Roads* [Mansfield, 1963].

[8] Sarah A. Dorsey, *Recollections of Henry Watkins Allen, Brigadier General Confederate States Army Ex-Governor of Louisiana* (New York and New Orleans, 1866), 263.

[9] *Ibid.*, 261.

the division and placed Colonel James R. Taylor of the 17th Texas in charge of the Texas brigade as its senior officer. To James Allen Hamilton of the 15th Texas it seemed "there was a continual roar of cannon and musketry," and the advance appeared to be checked for a moment. But the 34th Texas, left to support the Confederate artillery, pressed to the front and led the Texas brigade in a renewed charge which broke the Union line and took a Federal battery. The Texans then fired a volley into the flank of the Union troops facing Gray's brigade which provided the shock necessary to assist the Louisiana troops in capturing large numbers of the Federals. Walker's and Major's men also were advancing and the Union retreat became a rout. At dusk Federal reinforcements halted the Confederate surge along a small creek about three miles south. There, in one of the last volleys fired, the acting brigade commander, "the gallant Col. Taylor, Col. of the 17th Tex, fell, bravely leading his men against the enemy." It had been a hard fought battle and a smashing victory for Richard Taylor, but many units, among them the 17th Texas, were stunned by their losses.[10]

Polignac's and Walker's divisions followed Green's cavalry and the fresh Missouri and Arkansas infantry divisions of Generals Mosby M. Parsons and Thomas J. Churchill south toward Pleasant Hill on April 9. Federal troops held the village and Taylor formed his command for battle during the afternoon, hoping to destroy the Union army he had defeated on the 8th. Polignac's division was held in reserve on the Mansfield road because it had borne the heaviest fighting at Sabine Crossroads. Taylor's plan, to turn the Union left, seemed successful at first but the turning column was flanked suddenly and driven back. Taylor had already committed his center and left in a series of attacks and was forced to call on Polignac's division in an effort to relieve the pressure on the retreating Confederate right. The new division commander stood erect in his saddle, called to the decimated little division, "My boys, follow your Polignac," and led them down the road into line between Walker's men in the Southern center and Green's troopers on the Confederate left.[11] The fresh infantry drove back advanced Union lines and recovered some lost ground but confusion and

---

[10]*Ibid.*, 262; Hamilton Diary, April 8, 1864; Smith and Mullins, eds., "The Diary of H. C. Medford, Confederate Soldier, 1864," *Southwestern Historical Quarterly*, XXXIV, 218-219; report of Richard Taylor, April 18, 1864, *Official Records*, Series I, Vol. XXXIV, Pt. 1, 564-565; Combs, "Texas Boys in the War," *Confederate Veteran*, XXXV, 265; Bush, "Maj. William M. Bush," *ibid.*, VIII, 547; Thomas Reuben Bonner, "Sketches of the Campaign of 1864," *The Land We Love*, V, 466; Taylor, *Destruction and Reconstruction*, 196-197; Wooten, *Comprehensive History of Texas, 1685-1897*, II, 640-641.

[11] Blessington, *Walker's Texas Division*, 198; Galveston *Tri-Weekly News*, April 18, 1864.

darkness forced their recall as the day ended. A stalemate resulted from the fighting on the 9th which was resolved in favor of the Confederates when the Union army retreated to Grand Ecore on April 10.[12]

Losses in Polignac's Texas brigade had been heavy during the two days of combat, most coming at Sabine Crossroads on the 8th. The 15th Texas had suffered two killed and fourteen wounded; the 17th Texas twenty-three killed and forty-five wounded; the 22nd Texas four killed and thirty wounded; the 31st Texas three killed, twenty-five wounded, and one missing; and the 34th Texas seven killed and fifty-eight wounded, a total of 213 casualties.[13]

Polignac led his men back to their camps above Mansfield in easy marches on April 10 and 11. There on the 12th, the Texas brigade drew new canteens, cartridge boxes, belts, and bayonets from captured Union stores in preparation for a renewal of fighting. At the same time, Kirby Smith was considering the possibility of sending select infantry units, including Polignac's Texans, to aid General Sterling Price in Arkansas. On April 14, Smith decided to send instead Walker's, Parsons', and Churchill's divisions. Polignac's division, with its commander newly appointed a major general, was sent south to support the cavalry harassing Banks's retreat.[14]

The Texas brigade passed over both battlefields of the previous week during its march and camped below Pleasant Hill on the night of the 15th. After a day's rest, the Texans again marched toward Grand Ecore on the 17th, with newly promoted Colonel James Harrison in command after a hard ride from Texas and the official resignation of J. W. Speight on April 15. The brigade sent a mass letter to Taylor after Harrison's return requesting that the colonel of the 15th Texas be made their permanent brigade commander. A one day halt at Double Bridge was followed by a twenty-eight mile march to camps twelve miles from Natchitoches on the 19th. The next day the brigade retraced its march to Double Bridge, then moved back again on the 21st to within

---

[12] Hamilton Diary, April 9, 1864; report of Richard Taylor, April 18, 1864, *Official Records*, Series I, Vol. XXXIV, Pt. 1, 567-568; report of George W. Baylor, April 18, 1864, *ibid.*, 618; Hamilton P. Bee, "Battle of Pleasant Hill—An Error Corrected," *Southern Historical Society Papers*, VIII, 185; Taylor, *Destruction and Reconstruction*, 199-205; Wooten, *Comprehensive History of Texas, 1685-1897*, II, 641.

[13] Houston *Daily Telegraph*, April 20, 1864.

[14] E. Kirby Smith to R. Taylor, April 12, 1864, *Official Records*, Series I, Vol. XXXIV, Pt. 1, 531-532; Taylor to W. R. Boggs, April 14, 1864, *ibid.*, 533; General Orders No. 13, Headquarters Trans-Mississippi Department, April 13, 1864, *ibid.*, Series I, Vol. XXXIV, Pt. 3, 764; Taylor, *Destruction and Reconstruction*, 218; Record Book, Company F, 22nd Texas, April 10-14, 1864; Hamilton Diary, April 10-14, 1864.

seven miles of Natchitoches, still without engaging the enemy. At that point W. H. King, former colonel of the 18th Texas in Walker's division and a recently appointed brigadier general, was placed in command of the Texas brigade. Harrison subdued his own unhappiness at the decision and restrained another petition on his behalf by the brigade.[15] King was unable to assume command, however, because of a severe wound received at Sabine Crossroads. As a result the brigade was left under its senior colonel, Robert D. Stone of the 22nd Texas, a pre-war lawyer originally from Missouri.

The Texans cooked two days rations on April 22 and marched nine miles south in the afternoon. On the 23rd, Polignac's entire division pressed forward down the Cane River hoping to help close a trap around the Federal army as it retired from Grand Ecore toward Alexandria. Footsore and weary, the Texas infantry crossed the river and hurried through Cloutierville on the 24th past houses set ablaze by the retreating Federals. But they arrived too late, for the Confederate cavalry at Monett's Ferry had given way before superior numbers despite a strong position, and the Union forces had escaped. With the need to move rapidly removed, the Texans made a short march on the 25th and camped at the ferry.[16]

Polignac sent for Harrison about 2:00 A.M. on April 26

> and informed me [Harrison] that there was a gunboat aground up red River about twelve miles [near Montgomery] and three transports attending her. He wanted me to march immediately and attack them with My Regt [the 15th Texas.] I marched all night, found the distance 18 miles, and that the information was totally incorrect. There were three Iron clads, two Transports fitted up with guns, and one Transport with Sharpshooters.[17] I made my arrangements· to attack them immediately by surprise. I got a guide and marched my men by the flank noiselessly through the thick woods and under growth to within one hundred yards of the Bank when I came in to line of Battle by the motion of my sword and by the motion of the sword gave the order to advance. I marched in front with my six shooter. . . . My firing was to be the signal for a general Engagement. The surprise was complete. Thy [sic] Knew nothing of us atall [sic] until

15 *Ibid.*, April 14-21, 1864; Record Book, Company F, 22nd Texas, April 14-21, 1864; Muster Roll of the Field, Staff and Band, of the Fifteenth Regiment T. V. I., 31 August 1864 to 31 October 1864, Texas History Collection, Baylor University; Alwyn Barr, ed., "William T. Mechling's Journal of the Red River Campaign, April 7 - May 10, 1864," *Texana*, I, 371; Taylor, *Destruction and Reconstruction*, 218-219; J. E. Harrison to Dear Ballinger, April 16, 22, 1864, Ballinger Collection.

16 J. E. Harrison to Dear Ballinger, April 22, 1864, *ibid.;* Record Book, Company F, 22nd Texas, April 22-25, 1864; Hamilton Diary, April 22-24, 1864; report of R. Taylor, April 24, 1864, *Official Records*, Series I, Vol. XXXIV, Pt. 1, 579, 580; *Confederate Veteran*, XVI, 395; W. H. King, "Early Experiences in Missouri," *ibid.*, XVII, 502; Robert P. Mayo, "Colonel Robert Dillard Stone," *ibid.*, 359; Taylor, *Destruction and Reconstruction*, 220.

17 Union vessels present were the ironclad *Eastport,* the "tinclads" *Cricket, Juliet,* and *Fort Hindman,* and the pump boats *Champion No. 3* and *Champion No. 5.*

we opened on them [about 9.00 A.M.] They were wooding on the oposite [sic] Bank and plundering a Resedince [sic]. I selected a Big portly Captain sitting in a Big arm chair. When my pistol fired he tumbled out of his seat like a Turtle off a log, and through the hatch he went. My whole line opened at once. Such consternation I never saw. It was fully ten minutes before Thy [sic] could arrange themselves to fight, but when they did by going above and below us and in front, the shells and missles [sic] came like a hail storm. The whole Earth shook. Timber and Bushes were litterly [sic] torn to pieces. I made my men fire and fall flat on the ground and Load and shoot deliberately. We did them great damage, in Killed and wounded, during the Engagement. The Best Boat, a Large Ironclad Monster [the *Eastport*] in turning to give us a Brod [sic] side grounded so fast she could not get off, and we would not let her have help. She blew up, Shaking the Earth, and scattering her large timbers in some instances for two hundred yards on The Bank. She Burned, another in going off got aground and was fired and Burned, the woodend [sic] ones were litterly [sic] riddled by our Balls . . .

The 15th Texas lost one killed, five wounded, and two missing in the peculiar engagement.[18]

When Admiral David D. Porter finally extracted the remaining Union vessels from Harrison's surprise assault, they steamed downstream directly into another. At the mouth of the Cane River Lieutenant Colonel John H. Caudle with 200 men of the 34th Texas and Florian O. Cornay's field battery waylaid the fleet again. Extremely accurate fire from the St. Mary Cannoneers and from Caudle's sharpshooters ran one transport aground, drove the other transport and two gunboats back up river, and riddled the only gunboat that passed their position. On April 27, Caudle's command forced the other transport aground and shot up the remaining warships as they struggled past the well defended river bend. The 34th Texas suffered only one wounded in two days of action. Harrison and Caudle rejoined the brigade at Monett's Ferry that night.[19]

Polignac's division moved forward again in easy marches on the 28th and 29th to McNutt's Hill, fifteen miles from Alexandria. There the Texas infantry remained until May 1 when they marched five miles down Bayou Rapides, still west of Alexandria. A ten mile march toward Lecompte followed on the 2nd while Confederate cavalry under their newly appointed commander, Major General John A. Wharton, skirmished with the Union forces holding the

---

[18] J. E. Harrison to Dear Ballinger, April 27, 1864, Ballinger Collection (condensed version in Galveston *Tri-Weekly News*, May 18, 1864); Hamilton Diary, April 25, 1864. See also report of David D. Porter, April 28, 1864, *Official Records, Navies*, Series I, Vol. XXVI, 71-77.

[19] J. E. Harrison to Dear Ballinger, April 27, 1864, Ballinger Collection; report of R. Taylor, April 27, 1864, *Official Records*, Series I, Vol. XXXIV, Pt. 1, 583; report of David D. Porter, April 28, 1864, *Official Records, Navies*, Series I, Vol. XXVI, 71-77; Taylor, *Destruction and Reconstruction*, 222-223.

river town. On the 4th and 5th the Texans moved seventeen miles to Bayou Boeuf. A ten mile march on the 6th took them below Cheneyville, still on the Boeuf but within supporting distance of Major's cavalry, which was harassing the Union supply line up the Red River. The Texas infantry were up at 3:00 A.M. on the 7th to reach Lloyd's Bridge by eight o'clock that morning. There they halted until five o'clock in the afternoon when orders came to move on and camp at Lecompte. Polignac's Texans were hurried forward to Bayou Lamourie early on the morning of May 8 to aid Bagby's brigade in heavy skirmishing with part of Banks's army, which continued to hold Alexandria while working to pass Porter's fleet over the shallow rapids there. The Texas infantry then returned to their camps at Lecompte during the afternoon. On the 10th, orders took the brigade again up Bayou Lamourie where it lay in line of battle all day while the cavalry skirmished in front. A twelve mile march on the 11th brought the Texans to the Red River at dusk. The Texas regiments plodded on to Marksville on the 12th where they camped to the sound of heavy cannonading on the river.[20]

After a day in camp the brigade marched six miles on May 14 to Bayou de Glaize to harass the Union retreat which had resumed the day before.[21] At four o'clock on the afternoon of the 15th

> The "Long Roll" was sounded and Fall in Fall in was heard through the encampment. In a few minutes the line of march was taken up to meet the Enemy. We [Polignac's division] had gotten below them. Two miles and a half brought us on the Edge of a prairy [sic] about seven miles long (Through which the Road ran) by one [and] a half miles wide, at the Lower end of which in a small ravine, and among some scattered timber the Little Viliage [sic] of Mansura is nestled. Here in the Edge of the Timber we stopped on our arms, the Enemy had fallen Back. My [Harrison's] Bed was the great Earth, my pillow the root of a tree. My rest was sweet and refreshing. Day Dawned [on May 16, 1864,] and our yawn was saluted by the crackling of small arms in the Distance.[22] The little Ravine alluded to was some three or four hundred yds from the Main Timber. On this we had drawn up and posted 32 pieces [of] Artilary [sic], And to protect which our little Divission [sic] of Twenty five hundred men were drawn up in the open prairy [sic] to the rear. Directly Dark lines in the distance were visable [sic] reaching clear across the prairy [sic] and to the rear of which colum [sic] upon colum [sic] were seen advancing. All was quit [sic] and still as death excep [sic] the passing to and fro of officers giving orders. On the dark lines press[ed] until within 1000 yds, open prairy [sic], when all at once as if the heavens had been rent asunder thirty two pieces

---

[20] Reports of R. Taylor, May 6, 8, 1864, *Official Records*, Series I, Vol. XXXIV, Pt. 1, 588, 589; Record Book, Company F, 22nd Texas, April 28 - May 13, 1864; Hamilton Diary, April 28 - May 12, 1864.

[21] *Ibid.*, May 13-15, 1864; Record Book, Company F, 22nd Texas, May 13-15, 1864.

[22] Skirmishing became general about 6:00 A.M.

of our artilary [sic] opened upon them, Throwing them into confution [sic]. They retired But soon advanced with their entire force 30,000 Strong,[23] With Their artilary [sic] in front. Our little divission [sic] stood before them like a stone wall for two hours. The scene was grand and sublime beyond description. Language becomes poor when I attemt [sic] a description. An order comes to march[24]

and after four hours of effective bluffing Taylor withdrew his small army allowing the Union forces to continue on toward Simmesport at about 10:00 A.M.[25]

Polignac's division withdrew four miles to Bayou Rouge for the night. At ten o'clock the next morning the Texans turned east and proceeded ten miles along the bayou before nightfall. Near Norwood's Plantation on Yellow Bayou the Confederate cavalry began to press the Federal rear guard on May 18. The Texas brigade marched nine miles that morning and arrived between one and two o'clock in the afternoon.[26] The division of

Genl Polignac Came into line in the middle or across a large field, Extending from Bayou Deglaise [sic] far back in the swamp on the Right. Genl Wharton was Ranking officer and in command. Our [the Texas brigade's] position was a strong one though in an open field. We had the advantage of a large ditch with others to fall Back on. We remained here, for half an hour, our artillery just in front shelling (just in front of this field. The woods extend to the Bayou covered with thick undergrowth). When Genl Wharton ordered our line forward, we formed in another ditch two hundred yds in front of our first position, still a good one. When Genl Wharton ordered us forward to the woods, The La Brigade on the right . . . was moved off by the right flank leaving a wide gap between them and the Texas Brigade, two Regts of which was held in reserve (17th Consolidated and Hawpe's [31st Texas]). Caudle [with the 34th Texas] occupied [sic] the left near the levee, I [Harrison] with the 15th Texas occupied [sic] the center, Stone's Battalion [the 22nd Texas] the right. We advanced to the Edge of the field, the fence having been burned away. He[re] we were halted, in ten paces of a wall of thick undergrowth. I rode to Col Stone Comdg Brigade and asked him where he wanted my line formed. He seemed to be at a loss. I told him we had better fall Back to [the] deep ditch one hundred and fifty yds to the rear of us, throw out Skirmishers and feel for the Enemy. I believed them to be concealed just before us. He did not fall back but sent out Skirmishers. Thy [sic] had not advanced more than sixty steps before they were in ten feet of the 16th Army Corps, rising up in four lines and demanding their surrender. Some of them escaped and got Back, when the four lines were precipitated upon us, and the fight became desperate. Col Caudle's left did not reach the Leevee [sic], by one hundred yds, and between the high leave [sic] and the Bayou there was

<hr>

[23] The Union battle lines at Mansura actually contained about 18,000 men.

[24] J. E. Harrison to My Dear Daughter, May 18, 1864, Ballinger Collection.

[25] Report of R. Taylor, May 16, 1864, *Official Records*, Series I, Vol. XXXIV, Pt. 1, 593.

[26] Record Book, Company F, 22nd Texas, May 16-18, 1864; Hamilton Diary, May 16-18, 1864; J. E. Harrison to My Dear Daughter, May 18, 1864, to Dear Ballinger, May 22, 1864, Ballinger Collection.

a space of 40 yds, protected by the Leave [sic]. The Eney [sic] moved a flanking column up the Bayou. Caudle was soon overwhelmed, and was ordered to fall Back by Col Stone. I received no orders, and was engaging four lines to my front at a distance of 25 and thirty paces, Thy [sic] constantly demanding my surrender. I replied with Enfield Rifles, holding them steady. [We] cut down their flag Bearers twice, [but] Thy [sic] were promptly raised, and the demand repeated surrender you damned Rebels or we'l [sic] Kill you all. By this time Caudle had gone far to the rear, (Col Stone with his [Caudle's] command) and the Flanking Column opening a desperate Enfilading fire upon me there being now no troops between me and them. I yet had received no orders. J. H[arrison] seeing my condition dismounted his company between the Bayou and Levee, double quicked his company ¼ mile and attacked the head of this column so furiously that they fell Back. He did it to great advantage, his company filling up the space between the Leve [sic] and Bayou and could exibit [sic] as much front as the Eney [sic] though thy [sic] had six Regts. When this was done I fell Back, to the ditch alluded to and opened fire on [the Union] advance forcing them Back to the Bushes, and then met our reserve with the artilary [sic], when thy [sic] were driven Back entirely and we held the field[27]

Colonel Robert Stone, the brigade commander, was killed by a Minie ball while reporting to General Wharton, and again Harrison was in charge. The Texans, who had held their ground for four hours, then fell back a few miles just before dark to camps on Clear Bayou near Moreauville.[28] All remaining Union forces crossed the Atchafalaya that night, bringing the Red River campaign to an end.

Casualties in the Texas regiments confirmed all accounts of the hotly contested struggle. The 15th Texas had suffered twelve killed, thirty-seven wounded, and twenty-four missing; the 34th Texas had lost sixteen killed, forty-two wounded including Major William M. Bush, and sixty-two missing; and the 22nd Texas lost four killed including Colonel Stone, eight wounded, and two missing.[29] Thus the brigade casualties totaled 208 including thirteen officers. Wounded were cared for at Coco's Plantation on Bayou de Glaize in the slave quarters which were converted into a makeshift hospital. A consensus among the Confederate troops engaged at Yellow Bayou held that the battle had been unnecessary, since

[27] *Ibid.* See also report of R. Taylor, May 19, 1864, *Official Records*, Series I, Vol. XXXIV, Pt. 1, 594; report of R. W. Fyan, May 21, 1864, *ibid.*, 370.

[28] J. E. Harrison to My Dear Daughter, May 18, 1864, to Dear Ballinger, May 22, 1864, Ballinger Collection; Record Book, Company F, 22nd Texas, May 18, 1864; Mayo, "Colonel Robert Dillard Stone," *Confederate Veteran*, XVII, 359; Sioux to Ed. Telegraph, May 19, 1864, Houston *Daily Telegraph*, June 1, 1864.

[29] *Ibid.*, June 8, 1864. Harrison summarized the casualties of the 15th Texas as ten killed, forty-two wounded, and twenty-two missing. J. E. Harrison to My Dear Daughter, May 18, 1864, Ballinger Collection. See also Hamilton Diary, May 18, 1864.

the Federals were retreating across the Atchafalaya at the time, and placed the blame on General Wharton.[30] It would appear actually to have been a rather poorly managed effort to punish the Union army one last time before it escaped completely.

Harrison led his brigade back toward the battlefield on the evening of May 19 and the 22nd Texas buried Colonel Stone in a small church yard near the bayou. The Texans then remained in camp near Simmesport for ten days until the 29th when they moved three miles to new tenting grounds on Alligator Lake. There the infantry remained through June 8, undisturbed except by rain on the evening of the 1st.[31]

At the brigade camp on June 1, 1864, Colonel Harrison presented General Polignac with a horse from the officers of his former brigade. In his remarks on that occasion Harrison reaffirmed the officers' confidence in Polignac as a commander and their esteem of him as a gentleman and a true southerner. Polignac in reply expressed his appreciation for the gift, spoke of duty as the highest motivation for human action, and promised that if events allowed he would ride the "noble charger" across Texas after the war to see the men of his old brigade.[32]

Details from the brigade went on picket along the Atchafalaya but there was little excitement except for the capture of a field battery by Union gunboats on the 8th. Harrison brought the Texans back twenty miles toward Mansura on June 9, then in leisurely marches on the 10th and 11th to Marksville. While in camp there orders were issued for two hours of drill at 8:00 A.M. and two more at 2:00 P.M., time consuming but somewhat colorless tasks for men who so recently had defended the Trans-Mississippi Department successfully from invasion. On the 15th, Major George W. Merrick officially received command of the 22nd Texas, then reduced to battalion strength and organization.[33]

Kirby Smith had begun to contemplate an advance into Missouri immediately after the end of the Red River campaign. That idea quite possibly inspired the march of Harrison's brigade from Marks-

---

30 [W.] Randolph [Howell] to _____, May 21, 1864, Howell Collection, Archives, University of Texas Library; J. E. Harrison to Dear Ballinger, May 22, 1864, Ballinger Collection; D. R. Wallace to Mrs. Carter, [1864], photocopy, Tate Collection.

31 Record Book, Company F, 22nd Texas, May 19 - June 8, 1864; Hamilton Diary, May 19 - June 9, 1864; Mayo, "Colonel Robert Dillard Stone," Confederate Veteran, XVII, 359.

32 Houston Daily Telegraph, July 1, 1864.

33 George W. Guess to Mrs. Sarah H. Cockrell, June 18, 23, 30, 1864; Hamilton Diary, June 9-11, 1864; Record Book, Company F, 22nd Texas, June 8-26, 1864; R. Taylor to W. R. Boggs, June 8, 1864, Official Records, Series I, Vol. XXXIV, Pt. 4, 654-655.

ville twelve miles up the Red River beginning at 4:00 A.M. on July 4. The Texas infantry covered twenty-three miles during the next two days, crossed the river, and camped at Pineville on the 6th. Up again at four o'clock on the 7th, the Texans recrossed the river and marched eighteen miles to McNutt's Hill where they camped for three nights. From July 14 to 16 the brigade moved in easy stages to Lecompte, then five miles on the 17th to "Camp Boggs" on Beaver Creek. There Harrison rested and drilled his men while Kirby Smith in Shreveport considered new orders from General Braxton Bragg in Georgia, orders to send Walker's and Polignac's divisions across the Mississippi with recently promoted Lieutenant General Richard Taylor.[34]

As a result of the new orders Harrison's brigade marched fifteen miles toward Alexandria on July 29. Ten miles on the 30th took the Texans across the Red River again to Pineville where they remained for two days. On August 2, the march was renewed in the direction of Trinity. The Texas infantry covered fifty-five miles in four days to camp a mile below Trinity on the Black River. On the 6th, the Texans marched north to Harrisonburg, where they were welcomed warmly on the 7th as the former defenders of the town. Gray's brigade and Walker's division were camped there also, with pickets out on the Tensas and Black rivers and details entrenching the entire position. Harrison's brigade joined in those activities for the next two weeks, during which time Major George Merrick and Captain John A. Buck of the 22nd Texas were promoted to lieutenant colonel and major respectively.

Muttered protests over the proposed crossing of the Mississippi developed into stubborn opposition in August, 1864, among members of both infantry divisions who preferred to serve in defense of their home states. Two hundred men of Polignac's division deserted and Harrison admitted that "there has been a greadeal [sic] of excitement in my Brigade. I have lost 123 deserted, [who] won't cross the River. There are many others who dislike it extremely, . . ."[35] Kirby Smith suspended the attempt to cross troops

---

[34] W. R. Boggs to R. Taylor, July 28, 1864, *ibid.*, Series I, Vol. XLI, Pt. 1, 90; Joseph H. Parks, *General Edmund Kirby Smith, C.S.A.* (Baton Rouge, 1954), 419; J. E. Harrison to Dear Major Bryan, July 27, 1864, Bryan Collection; Muster Roll, Company D, 15th Regiment of Texas Volunteer Infantry, 30 June 1864 to 31 August 1864, in possession of Robert W. Glover, Tyler, Texas; Hamilton Diary, July 4-7, 1864; Record Book, Company F, 22nd Texas, July 9-29, 1864.

[35] *Ibid.*, July 29 - August 19, 1864; J. E. Harrison to My Dear Son, August 21, 1864, Harrison Papers; Harrison to My Dear Ballinger, August 13, 1864, Ballinger Collection; George W. Guess to Mrs. S. H. Cockrell, August 16, 1864; Washita to Dear Herald, August 16, 1864, Dallas *Herald,* September 10, 1864; S. B. Buckner to W. R. Boggs, August 20, September 3, 1864, *Official Records,* Series I, Vol. XLI, Pt. 1, 113, 120.

on August 22 because Union gunboats controlled the river and the morale of the troops involved had become seriously impaired.[36]

From a camp on Sicily Island Harrison's brigade made short marches to Deer Creek and Lake Louis between August 26 and 29. Then, on the 30th, Walker's and Polignac's divisons began an extended march north to reinforce Major General John B. Magruder, the newly appointed district commander for Arkansas. The Texas brigade proceeded to the Boeuf River on the 31st, rested for two days, and continued on to Columbia on the Ouachita River by September 2. Harrison's men covered thirty-two miles on the 3rd and 4th to arrive near Monroe on the second night. The Texans marched through Monroe on the 5th and camped north of town almost a week. Two hours of drill on the 6th, a heavy rain during the 7th, and the execution of a deserter from the 34th Texas on the 9th were the events of note for a period which also saw the brigade's sick list increase steadily despite the arrival of quinine.[37]

The week in camp ended abruptly on September 13, when Magruder ordered both divisions to Monticello, Arkansas, in anticipation of a Federal advance from Pine Bluff. Harrison's brigade moved north by forced marches through Bastrop, Louisiana, along Bayou Bartholomew, and crossed the Arkansas line on the 15th. The Texans continued through Hamburg on the 17th to camps on the 18th near Magruder's headquarters at Monticello. Surgeon David Wallace of the 15th Texas pronounced the region

> as poor as poverty to begin with, foraged upon by a large body of troops, quartered here for a month, the prospect for something to sustain man and beast do not look promising. We are getting very poor rations for ourselves, our animals worse. We are getting ten ears of corn per day for our horses. This, as well as the meal we eat, has to be transported sixty miles. From present indications, if a campaign is attempted here, our saddle horses will starve before spring.

Despite such dismal prospects, Harrison inspected the brigade on the 22nd in preparation for a review of the entire army by Magruder. Polignac's division was paraded along with Walker's,

[36] W. R. Boggs to Lieutenant General Taylor, August 22, 1864, *ibid.*, 117. For a complete discussion of the transfer efforts see Parks, *General Edmund Kirby Smith*, 420-428.

[37] Muster Roll of the Field, Staff and Band, of the Fifteenth Regiment T. V. I., 31 August 1864 to 31 October 1864, Texas History Collection, Baylor University; Washita to Dear Herald, September 11, 1864, Dallas *Herald*, September 24, 1864; Blessington, *Walker's Texas Division*, 273, 275; Record Book, Company F, 22nd Texas, August 24 - September 13, 1864; Muster Roll, Company D, 15th Regiment of Texas Volunteer Infantry, 30 June 1864 to 31 August 1864, in possession of Robert W. Glover, Tyler, Texas.

Churchill's, and Parsons' on September 26 and "Prince John" reviewed his men at a gallop.[38]

Magruder sent his infantry west on October 1, to place them in position for a diversion in favor of Major General Sterling Price's cavalry returning from a raid into Missouri or for defensive operations against a Union advance south from Little Rock. The new marching orders took the Texans to Warren on the 2nd in a heavy rain and on through heavily timbered southern Arkansas on the 6th to Camden. The Texas regiments helped entrench the town on the 7th, then moved on to Washington on the 8th and to nearby Camp Bragg two days later. On the 13th and 14th, the brigade retraced its steps to Camden as Magruder contemplated an attack on the reduced Federal garrison at Little Rock. While the movement to Camden was underway another change was effected; Brigadier General Wilburn Hill King for a second time was appointed brigade commander despite efforts by Polignac, Wharton, and Walker to have Harrison promoted and permanently assigned to the brigade. Kirby Smith requested the promotion and suggested to the War Department King's transfer to leave a place for Harrison. There were no immediate results.[39] King, a big man with a dark complexion, black hair and eyes, originally had come to Texas from Georgia in 1856. While in Missouri in 1861, he had enlisted in the Missouri State Guard under Price, but he had returned to Texas to join the Confederate army in 1862. He had led the 18th Texas at Bayou Bourbeau, thus he was not totally unknown to the brigade, nor was he personally disliked by its members.[40] Harrison had finally reached the end of his patience with

---

[38] David R. Wallace to R. C. Burleson, in Duncan, "David Richard Wallace," *Texana*, I, 346; Record Book, Company F, 22nd Texas, September 13-26, 1864; Muster Roll of the Field, Staff and Band, of the Fifteenth Regiment T. V. I., 31 August 1864 to 31 October 1864, Texas History Collection, Baylor University; Blessington, *Walker's Texas Division*, 278; J. W. Lewis to the Commanding Officer of Infantry at Monroe, September 9, 13, 1864, *Official Records*, Series I, Vol. XLI, Pt. 3, 916-917, 927-928.

[39] J. B. Magruder to W. R. Boggs, September 15, 1864, *ibid.*, 932-934; E. Kirby Smith to Magruder, October 3, 1864, *ibid.*, 978-979; Magruder to Kirby Smith, October 12, 1864, *ibid.*, 1003; Blessington, *Walker's Texas Division*, 279, 280; William W. Heartsill, *Fourteen Hundred and 91 Days in the Confederate Army* (1876; reprint ed. by Bell I. Wiley, Jackson, 1954), 22; J. E. Harrison to My Dear Ballinger, September 12, 1864, Ballinger Collection; Harrison to My Dear Son, September 12, October 8, 1864, Harrison Papers; Record Book, Company F, 22nd Texas, October 1 - November 13, 1864; Muster Roll of the Field, Staff and Band, of the Fifteenth Regiment T. V. I., 31 August 1864 to 31 October 1864, Texas History Collection, Baylor University.

[40] Wilburn Hill King, Autobiographies, King Papers, United Daughters of the Confederacy Museum, Austin; King, "Early Experiences in Missouri," *Confederate Veteran*, XVII, 502-503; L. T. Wheeler, "Gen. Wilbur[n] Hill King," *ibid.*, XIX, 172-173; L. E. Daniell, comp., *Personnel of the Texas State Government, with Sketches of Distinguished Texans* . . . (Austin, 1887), 26-28.

the government, however, and determined to exert such influence as was available to him to effect the oft expected promotion. On November 1, 1864, he left for Richmond, ostensibly to discuss Indian affairs, though primarily equipped with documents and letters about his qualifications from fellow officers to their friends in Congress as well as a letter from Kirby Smith to President Jefferson Davis.[41]

As a result of the extended marches in September and October and a continuing shortage of tents and blankets, sick lists in Polignac's division had lengthened and its strength fell to 1,132 privates in mid-October. Another indication of the reduced size of the Texas brigade lay in the fact that Captain M. M. Singletary was then in command of the 17th Texas, which had lost all of its field grade officers in the Red River campaign. Finally, in late October and early November, the Texans were allowed to rest and recuperate in camps near Camden, although they also spent time working on the town's fortifications with some variety supplied by drill periods.[42]

Magruder decided to disperse his infantry for the winter in early November, thus allowing them more room in which to forage. Polignac's division was ordered on the 13th to Walnut Hill near the Red River in Lafayette County, Arkansas. Steady marches of from ten to sixteen miles a day brought the Texas brigade to its destination by November 19. The Texans' stay proved to be a short one. Kirby Smith had decided to recall the divisions of Polignac and Major General John H. Forney (formerly Walker's) since there was little danger of winter operations in Arkansas and supplies were more abundant in Louisiana. King received his marching orders on the 21st and proceeded south through Rocky Mount across Bayou Bodcau to Minden, Louisiana, in six days. The Texas regiments passed through the town on November 26 and set up permanent winter camps three miles east.[43]

King's brigade spent December primarily in camp with details at work on the road from Minden to Shreveport. The men were

[41] J. E. Harrison to My Dear Son, November 1, 1864, Harrison Papers; John R. Baylor to James A. Seddon, December 21, 1864, *Official Records*, Series IV, Vol. III, 961.

[42] Organization of the Army of the Trans-Mississippi Department, September 30, 1864, *ibid.*, Series I, Vol. XLI, Pt. 3, 967; Edmund P. Turner to Major Rowley, October 18, 1864, *ibid.*, Series I, Vol. XLI, Pt. 4, 1002; Muster Roll, Company E, 15th Texas Infantry, 31 August 1864 to 31 October 1864, photocopy, Tate Collection; Record Book, Company F, 22nd Texas, October 15 - November 30, 1864.

[43] *Ibid.*, November 13-27, 1864; J. Bankhead Magruder to Major General Forney, November 7, 1864, *Official Records*, Series I, Vol. XLI, Pt. 4, 1033; S. S. Anderson to Magruder, November 16, 1864, *ibid.*, 1052; E. Kirby Smith to S. B. Buckner, November 29, 1864, *ibid.*, 1082.

well pleased on the whole with their new brigade commander, perhaps to some degree because the rations and health of the brigade held up well after the return to Louisiana. On the 2nd, three deserters from the 15th Texas were shot. Life in camp then returned to normal until the 7th when Polignac reviewed the division near Minden. The weather, which had been pleasant and cool, turned to rain on the 16th and it continued for four days. On the 20th, the contrasts of camp life stood out sharply. W. S. Douglas of the 34th Texas noted that "A revival of religion has commenced in camps. All take an interest [in] it. I never saw such a difference in men in my life." Cursing had fallen off considerably and over two-hundred-fifty men had been converted since that summer. Meanwhile, W. J. Notley of the 22nd Texas recorded on the same day, with apparent distaste, that there was "Plenty of whisky in Company [F]." The 17th Texas had reason to be pleased, however, for in December the regiment acquired a new colonel, Thomas F. Tucker, a Mexican War veteran who had risen from lieutenant in 1861.[44]

---

[44] Abstract from return of the Army of the Trans-Mississippi Department, for the month of December, 1864, *ibid.*, 1140; W. S. Douglas to Dear Sister, December 20, 1864, Civil War Biographical File; Record Book, Company F, 22nd Texas, December 1-31, 1864; Muster Roll, Company E, 1st Texas Mounted Rifles, Mexican War, National Archives, photostat in possession of Cooper K. Ragan, Houston, Texas; Thomas F. Tucker Carded File, War Department Collection of Confederate Records, National Archives.

Chapter IV

# "A little soap and a chew of old flat"

## Texas, 1865

In January, 1865, drill was stepped up to one hour of company drill in the morning and two hours of battalion drill in the afternoon. General King drilled the entire brigade on the 3rd, one mile east of camp. On the 4th and 6th, march orders were issued but abandoned because of rain, and the Texans remained at Minden through the 12th. At 9:00 A. M. on the 13th, Polignac's division moved south toward Natchitoches. King's men had covered approximately sixty-five miles by January 17 when they camped at Grabbs Bluff just upstream on the Red River from Grand Ecore. There they remained until the 24th. The Texans then marched down to Grand Ecore, established new winter camps, and began work on the town's fortifications. Camp life on the Red River, interspersed with rain and entrenching, continued through February, 1865.[1]

Elsewhere changes were in the planning stage, for a shortage of forage forced Kirby Smith to dismount nine cavalry regiments in February. Two new infantry brigades were to be formed under William Steele and James E. Harrison, who had just returned from Richmond with a brigadier's wreath around the stars on his collar. Harrison was sent to Houston, Texas, on February 7 to assist Wharton in dismounting the cavalry. King's brigade was ordered split on the 16th to provide a hard core of trained infantry around which to create the new brigades. A change of orders at the same time left King in charge of one brigade and Harrison the other.[2]

No immediate action was taken, however, except to order the Texas regiments into Texas on the 20th. After a week's delay, the Texas brigade, minus the 34th Texas which was retained for King's new brigade, began the movement west on March 1. The Texans

---

[1] Record Book, Company F, 22nd Texas, January 1 - February 28, 1865; A. L. Nelms to M. J. Nelms, Mary B. and J. A. Nelms, February 18, 1865, Weddle Collection.

[2] S. Cooper to E. Kirby Smith, December 23, 1864, *Official Records,* Series I, Vol. XLI, Pt. 4, 1122; J. F. Belton to S. B. Buckner, February 7, 1865, *ibid.,* Series I, Vol. XLVIII, Pt. 1, 1371; Belton to John A. Wharton, February 7, 1865, *ibid.,* 1371-1372; W. R. Boggs to Buckner, February 16, 1865, *ibid.,* 1390.

passed through Pleasant Hill on the 4th, and camped on the 7th at Logansport on the Sabine River. After crossing into Texas on March 8, the brigade continued west to Mount Enterprise on the 11th and Rusk on the 15th, reaching Palestine by March 18. The Texas infantry rested for a day, then marched on through Centerville on the 23rd to a camp on the 25th below Madisonville. Anderson was left behind on the 27th, and after camping in a swamp on the 29th the footsore Texans plodded into Hempstead on March 30.[3]

General Polignac also passed through Texas in March, 1865, having been granted a leave of absence from his division to arouse sympathy and support for the Southern cause in France. Thus the Texas brigade and its most renowned commander left Louisiana, the scene of their greatest successes, at approximately the same time.[4]

While the brigade marched to Hempstead, Harrison had remained in Houston to assist Wharton, but once he had been officially assigned as its commander he hurried north on March 17 to join his troops, who numbered 1,082 officers and men. Once the brigade had reached Hempstead, Harrison returned to Houston to assist in organizing the division which would include his men. There, on April 6, he narrowly escaped injury while trying to stop the fatal shooting of Wharton by Colonel George W. Baylor in the Fannin Hotel. Harrison's brigade escorted Wharton's body from Hempstead to his nearby plantation on the 7th, through a dismal rain, a setting which epitomized the state of the Confederacy in the spring of 1865.[5]

On that same day, Harrison's brigade was ordered split to form the basis of Major General Sam B. Maxey's new infantry division. The 15th and the 17th Texas were to form a nucleus for the 1st Brigade which was also to include two newly dismounted cavalry units, Colonel James B. Likens' 35th Texas and Lieutenant Colonel Peter Hardeman's battalion. The 2nd Brigade was to include the 22nd Texas and the 31st Texas, plus the recently dismounted cavalry regiments of Colonels John P. Border and David S. Terry. In Maxey's absence, Harrison was ordered to assume command

---

[3] Record Book, Company F, 22nd Texas, February 20 - March 31, 1865; Blessington, *Walker's Texas Division*, 291.

[4] C. J. Polignac, "Polignac's Mission," *Southern Historical Society Papers*, XXXII, 365-371.

[5] Record Book, Company F, 22nd Texas, April 1-7, 1865; William Pitt Ballinger Diary, March 17, April 9, 1865, typescript, Archives, University of Texas Library; J. E. Harrison to Dear Ballinger, April 2, 1865, Ballinger Collection; Special Orders No. 75, Headquarters, District of Texas &c, March 16, 1865, *Official Records*, Series I, Vol. XLVIII, Pt. 1, 1427; Abstract from return of Harrison's brigade, March, 1865, *ibid.*, 1458.

and concentrate both brigades near Harrisburg. The troops of his old brigade arrived from Hempstead on the 11th by rail and immediately went into camp. On April 15, the 20th Texas Infantry under Colonel Henry M. Elmore replaced the 35th Texas Cavalry in the 1st Brigade, Brigadier General H. P. Bee was assigned to command the 2nd Brigade, and Brigadier General J. B. Robertson was given an even newer 3rd Brigade. The division, or such units as were present, shifted its camps five miles up the Hempstead railroad on the 17th, then stood for review on the 18th and 19th by officers who had escaped the Confederate surrenders east of the Mississippi.[6]

The 34th Texas had been included in the organization of King's new brigade, in late February and early March at Natchitoches and Shreveport, Louisiana, along with the 16th and the 18th Texas Infantry, and the 28th and Wells' Texas Dismounted Cavalry. As a part of Forney's division, the men of the 34th Texas had been ordered to Texas on March 5. The Texans had arrived on April 15 near Hempstead where they cleared ground for a camp and resumed daily drills.[7]

Maxey's new division still had not been fully organized by April 24 when a mass meeting of "Harrison's Brigade" was held at Camp Rogers. Harrison delivered a "brief, eloquent and well-timed address" on the purpose of the meeting. Then a committee of eight, representing the 15th, the 17th, the 22nd, and the 31st Texas, drafted resolutions which expressed faith in the Confederate cause, promised continued service by the brigade, and condemned desertion as treason. The resolutions were unanimously adopted. General Maxey assumed command of the division on April 25, exhorted his men to remain in the ranks with good spirits and steady discipline, and pointed "with pride and pleasure to the resolution of Harrison's Brigade." Yet Harrison admitted in private that "Our country is overwhelmed in gloom at our recent disasters—on the other side of the River."[8]

The last week in April proved a busy one for Maxey's division. General Magruder, who had returned to command the District of Texas in the spring of 1865, reshuffled the new units being added

---

[6] Special Orders No. 97, Headquarters, District of Texas &c., April 7, 1865, *ibid.*, Series I, Vol. XLVIII, Pt. 2, 1266; Special Orders No. 105, Headquarters, District of Texas, New Mexico, and Arizona, April 15, 1865, *ibid.*, 1281; Record Book, Company F, 22nd Texas, April 10-19, 1865.

[7] A. L. Nelms to M. J. Nelms, February 28, April 20, 1865, Weddle Collection; Blessington, *Walker's Texas Division*, 291-292, 294, 297, 302.

[8] Dallas *Herald*, May 11, 1865; General Orders No. 1, Headquarters Maxey's Infantry Division, April 25, 1865, W. S. Oldham Collection, Archives, University of Texas Library; J. E. Harrison to My Dear Bryan, April 25, 1865, Bryan Collection.

to the division, spread the brigades in strategic positions around Houston, then contemplated a shift of Harrison's brigade to Brownsville to hold the Rio Grande open to Southern trade.[9]

While the eastern armies of the Confederacy were breaking up during April and May, 1865, a fatalistic calm settled over the better disciplined units in the Trans-Mississippi Department. Maxey reviewed his division on May 10, and the Houston *Daily Telegraph* carried a letter on May 12 from a member of Company C, 15th Texas Infantry, announcing to the citizens of the city that the regiment was devoid of tobacco and soap. The correspondent then asked "Now see here, Mr. Editor, don't you think they '*orter*' give us a little soap and a *chew* of old flat?"[10] On May 14, Harrison's and Bee's brigades were ordered to Richmond, Texas. A week later both commands were ordered back through Houston to Navasota by rail. Apparently the railroads of Texas had failed at that point, for Harrison's brigade was still in Richmond on May 24, 1865. On that day Harrison issued his final order with the full approval of district headquarters, commanding the regimental officers to march their troops as near home as possible and to discharge them.[11] Most of the men of Forney's division, which included the 34th Texas, had accepted ultimate defeat by May 19 and had gone home of their own accord. The remaining troops of the division had been discharged on the 20th.[12] Thus, without fanfare or even the bitter memory of a mass surrender, the men who had made up Polignac's Texas Brigade trudged homeward.[13]

Many memories did accompany the small groups or individual veterans of the Texas brigade as they broke ranks for the last time. Faintly recalled were the stirring cavalry charges at Shirley's Ford and Newtonia, and the cries of the wounded in the burning haystacks at Prairie Grove. Less dim was the fearful cold of the

[9] Record Book, Company F, 22nd Texas, April 29-30, 1865; T. M. Jack to S. B. Maxey, April 25, 1865, *Official Records*, Series I, Vol. XLVIII, Pt. 2, 1286; Special Orders No. 116, Headquarters, District of Texas &c, April 26, 1865, *ibid.*, 1287; Special Orders No. 118, Headquarters District of Texas, New Mexico, and Arizona, April 28, 1865, *ibid.*, 1291; J. B. Magruder to E. Kirby Smith, April 28, 1865, *ibid.*, 1289-1291.

[10] Houston *Daily Telegraph*, May 10, 12, 1865.

[11] William T. Carrington to Major General Maxey, May 14, 1865, *Official Records*, Series I, Vol. XLVIII, Pt. 2, 1303; Special Orders No. 140, Headquarters District of Texas &c, May 20, 1865, *ibid.*, 1315; General Orders No. 13, Headquarters Harrison's Brigade, May 24, 1865, *ibid.*, 1318-1319; Yeary, *Reminiscences of the Boys in Gray*, 145.

[12] Blessington, *Walker's Texas Division*, 307; Wooten, *Comprehensive History of Texas, 1685-1897*, II, 640; A. L. Nelms to M. J. Nelms, April 29, 1865, Weddle Collection.

[13] J. E. Harrison to Andrew Johnson, June 23, 1865, photocopy, Tate Collection.

winter march through the Indian Territory, the steaming heat of Louisiana swamps, the incessant rain and bottomless mud at Stirling's Plantation, and the confusion of woods and ditches at Bayou Bourbeau. Most vivid of all were the explosions of huge gunboat shells along the banks of the Mississippi, the Ouachita, and the Red rivers, the staggering Union volleys at Mansfield, the sundown charge at Pleasant Hill, and the stand-up, no-quarter, fire fight along Yellow Bayou. Well over a hundred men, perhaps two hundred, had been killed on those fields and dozens of others had died of disease and cold in camp and on the march. Perhaps four or five hundred more carried home the scars of combat. An untold number of others, who were already home, bore a different mark, the figurative scar of a deserter. Those men and others like them, whatever their reasons for unauthorized absence, had been probably the most costly losses of all to Polignac's brigade and to the Southern war effort as a whole. Memories of the war, both good and bad, were to be lasting; but in late May, 1865, they were reluctantly given second place behind thoughts of fields turned to weeds which needed plowing, of offices and shops long closed which needed painting and dusting, and of a state worn down by war which needed rebuilding.

# The Battle of Bayou Bourbeau

Only one poem is known to exist written by a member of Polignac's Brigade about its service in the war. With sometimes awkward phrases, and a mixture of pride, sorrow, and thankfulness for survival—the emotions of a man who has recently been in combat—M. W. Oldham of the 15th Texas Infantry penned these lines after the battle of Bayou Bourbeau.

## Poetry Made to The Battle of Bordeaux Lea
*Which was fought 8 miles below Opelousas, Lea, Nov. 3d 1863*

Could I have Stood where Tom Green Stood amidst the Battle Roar
I could have saw what he then Saw perhaps a little more
Though I had enough to do to watch what I could See
For Yankee bombs and minie balls come whizing fast by me

Into the fight we went with cheerful Hearts Remembering what
    we swore
That we would live as Freemen live or fight forever more
They saw that we intended there that day to drive them out or
    die
And some of our brave Heroes did fall and bleed and die

The time had come when every man who had an eye could see
Upon that awful field who a freeman wished to be
We dreaded not their whizing bombs more than the falling leaves
We were fighting for our rights and to drive out old Lincoln's
    thieves

We fought for three long hours before the strife was o'er
We thought of home and loved ones perhaps we'd nea'r see more
We thought of our freedom perhaps we'd live to gain
And thought of our brave Comrads that fell among the slain

The loved ones now of those that fell upon the field that day
Are weeping in their lonely homes in secret graves they pray
That God may ever save their souls eternally in Heaven
That they in a comeing day to their loved ones be given

And may they ever praise their God in that Bright world above
And Spend vast Eternity in Joy and Peace and Love
Oh God forbid that ever I again that awful may see
My friends and fellow comrads dying arround me

And now may we and the Friend we've left behind
All meet once more on earth in love and peace of mind
Oh may this dreadful War Soon end and all be Peace again
And ever in our sunny south may we in peace remain

But now to the Battle Field our tearful Eyes we turn
And think of what we saw our hearts within us burn
To see what we passed through in that hour of distress
Oh! in every hour of that Kind I hope that God will bless

And now to all that this may see and all who read the same
Give Praise and honor and all that's due a Texan's name
And thanks to God who stood by and lent a helping hand
In gaining a great Victory to our little Texan Band

The above was Composed by M. W. Oldham.
Company "H" 15th T. V. I.*

---

* James Allen Hamilton Diary, 1861-1864.

# BIBLIOGRAPHY

## MANUSCRIPTS

A. M. Alexander Carded File, War Department Collection of Confederate Records, National Archives, Washington, D. C.

William Pitt Ballinger Collection, Archives, University of Texas Library. Included in these papers are thirty letters from James E. Harrison which span the entire war period.

William Pitt Ballinger Diary, 1864-1868, typescript, Archives, University of Texas Library.

Guy M. Bryan Collection, Archives, University of Texas Library. These papers also include several Harrison letters.

John H. Caudle Carded File, War Department Collection of Confederate Records, National Archives, Washington, D. C.

Civil War Biographical File, Archives, University of Texas Library. This file contains letters from A. C. Hill and W. S. Douglas of Polignac's brigade.

Confederate Muster Rolls, Archives, Texas State Library. Six muster rolls of the 31st Texas Cavalry are included in this collection.

Index to Compiled Service Records of Confederate Soldiers Who Served in Organizations from the State of Texas, microfilm, Archives, Texas State Library; originals in National Archives, Washington, D. C.

List of Military Organizations Carded by the Record and Pension Office, Confederate, Texas Lists, 1-241, Record Group No. 94, National Archives, photostat, Archives, Texas State Library.

Henry W. Dailey Collection, Archives, University of Texas Library. Contained in this collection are muster rolls of Company C, 31st Texas Cavalry, and a typescript of the D. D. Whetston Day Book, November, 1862 - February, 1864, which was kept by a member of the 31st Texas.

Eighth Census, 1860, Returns of Schedule 1, Free Inhabitants, Texas, microfilm, University of Texas Library.

Benjamin H. Epperson Collection, Archives, University of Texas Library. Included is an 1861 Robert H. Taylor letter.

Muster Rolls, Fifteenth Texas Infantry, Texas History Collection, Baylor University. This collection contains muster rolls of Companies A - I and a muster roll of the field and staff officers and the regimental band of the 15th Texas.

Muster Roll, Company D, 15th Regiment of Texas Volunteer Infantry, 30 June 1864 to 31 August 1864, in possession of Robert W. Glover, Tyler, Texas.

Civil War Letters, Guess to Cockrell, photostats, Archives, University of Texas Library. These are primarily letters from George W. Guess.

James Allen Hamilton Diary, 1861-1864, Archives, University of Texas Library. Hamilton was a member of the 15th Texas.

Harrison Papers, Texas History Collection, Baylor University. This collection includes a number of letters written during the war by James E. Harrison to his family.

W. R. Howell Collection, Archives, University of Texas Library.

Josephus S. Irvine Papers in possession of Jesse J. Lee, Houston, Texas.

John R. King Collection, Archives, Texas State Library.

Wilburn Hill King Papers, United Daughters of the Confederacy Museum, Austin, Texas.

W. S. Oldham Collection, Archives, University of Texas Library.

Elijah P. Petty Papers, Mansfield Battle Park Museum, Mansfield, Louisiana.

Camille de Polignac Diary, 1863-1864, microfilm, Russell Library, Northwestern State College of Louisiana. Permission to make limited use of the diary was granted by the Russell Library and by Roy Hatton who is to edit it.

David M. Ray Collection, Archives, University of Texas Library.

Oran M. Roberts Collection, Archives, University of Texas Library. Roberts' papers include a copy of his official report and other correspondence pertaining to the battle of Bayou Bourbeau.

Ashley W. Spaight Collection, Archives, University of Texas Library.

James G. Stevens Carded File, War Department Collection of Confederate Records, National Archives, Washington, D. C.

Mrs. C. B. Tate Collection, Archives, University of Texas Library. This collection contains photocopies of letters from James E. Harrison, J. W. Speight, and D. R. Wallace, as well as a muster roll of Company E, 15th Texas Infantry.

Speech of Robert H. Taylor, delivered in the House of Representatives, . . . upon the joint resolutions to recognize or approve the Convention to assemble 28th of January, 1861, Broadside, Archives, University of Texas Library.

Muster Roll, Company G, Thirty-fourth Texas Dismounted Cavalry, June 30, 1863, photostat, Archives, University of Texas Library; original in National Archives, Washington, D. C.

Thomas F. Tucker Carded File, War Department Collection of Confederate Records, National Archives, Washington, D. C.

Record Book, J. A. Buck's Company [F], Stevens' [22nd Texas Cavalry] Regiment, December, 1863 - April, 1865, photostat, Archives, University of Texas Library; original in possession of Llewellyn Notley, Teague, Texas.

Montee Nelms Weddle Collection, Archives, University of Texas Library. This collection contains the Civil War letters of A. L. Nelms, a member of the 34th Texas. Permission to use the letters was granted by the donor, Robert S. Weddle.

## NEWSPAPERS

Clarksville *Standard*, 1856, 1861-1863.

Dallas *Herald*, 1861-1865.

Houston *Daily Telegraph*, 1864-1865.

Houston *Tri-Weekly Telegraph*, 1863.

Waco *Tribune-Herald*, October 30, 1949, July 19, 1953.

## BOOKS AND ARTICLES

### I. Primary Sources

Acheson, Sam and Julie Ann Hudson O'Connell, eds., "George Washington Diamond's Account of the Great Hanging at Gainesville, 1862," *Southwestern Historical Quarterly*, LXVI, 331-414.

Barr, Alwyn, ed., "William T. Mechling's Journal of the Red River Campaign, April 7-May 10, 1864," *Texana*, I, 363-379.

Barrett, Thomas, *The Great Hanging at Gainesville, Cooke County, Texas, A. D. 1862.* Gainesville, 1885; reprinted Austin: Texas State Historical Association, 1961.

Bartlett, Napier, *Military Record of Louisiana; Including Biographical and Historical Papers Relating to the Military Organization of the State.* New Orleans: L. Graham and Co., 1875. Included is the diary of A. W. Hyatt of the Louisiana brigade in Polignac's division.

Bee, Hamilton P., "Battle of Pleasant Hill—An Error Corrected," *Southern Historical Society Papers*, VIII, 184-186.

Blessington, Joseph P., *The Campaigns of Walker's Texas Division* . . . . New York: Lange, Little and Co., 1875.

Bonner, Thomas Reuben, "Sketches of the Campaign of 1864," *The Land We Love*, V, 459-466, VI, 7-12.

Bush, Walter H., "Maj. William M. Bush," *Confederate Veteran,* VIII, 546-547.

"Camp Daniel Near Tyler, Texas Sept. 7, 1862," *Chronicles of Smith County,* II, 16.

Combs, D. S., "Texas Boys in the War," *Confederate Veteran,* XXXV, 265.

Cushing, E. H., pub., *The New Texas School Reader Designed For the Use of Schools in Texas.* Houston, 1864; reprinted Austin: The Steck Company, 1962. Included is an article on the battle of Bayou Fordoche.

DeLeon, T. C., *Belles, Beaux and Brains of the 60's.* New York: G. W. Dillingham Company, 1909.

Dorsey, Sarah A., *Recollections of Henry Watkins Allen, Brigadier General Confederate States Army Ex-Governor of Louisiana.* New York and New Orleans: M. Doolady, 1866. This volume contains detailed information on the battle of Mansfield, some of which probably was provided by Captain W. Eggeling of Polignac's staff whose assistance the author acknowledged.

Duncan, Merle Mears, ed., "An 1864 Letter to Mrs. Rufus C. Burleson," *Southwestern Historical Quarterly,* LXIV, 369-372.

Edwards, John N., *Shelby and His Men, or The War in the West.* Cincinnati: Miami Printing Co., 1867.

Erath, Lucy A., ed., *The Memoirs of Major George B. Erath, 1813-1891.* Waco: Heritage Society of Waco, 1956.

Green, Thomas, "Battle of Atchafalaya River," *Southern Historical Society Papers,* III, 62-63.

Grisamore, Silas, "Reminiscences," *Weekly Thibodaux Sentinel,* 1869.

Heartsill, William W., *Fourteen Hundred and 91 Days in the Confederate Army.* Marshall, 1876; reprint ed. by Bell I. Wiley, Jackson: McCowat-Mercer Press, 1954.

Hewitt, J. E., *1864 Battle of Mansfield, Mansfield, Louisiana . . .* Mansfield, 1925; reprint Mansfield: Kate Beard Chapter No. 397 Daughters of the Confederacy, 1949.

Johnson, Sidney Smith, *Texans Who Wore the Gray.* Tyler, 1907. Includes soldiers' reminiscences and biographical sketches.

King, W. H., "Early Experiences in Missouri," *Confederate Veteran,* XVII, 502-503.

Liddell, [St. John R.], "Trans-Mississippi and Spanish Fort," *Southern Bivouac* (New Series), II, 736-740.

Mayo, Robert P., "Colonel Robert Dillard Stone," *Confederate Veteran,* XVII, 359.

Moore, Frank E., ed., *The Rebellion Record: A Diary of American Events* . . . . 12 vols. New York: D. Van Nostrand Publisher, 1861-1868.

Noel, Theophilus, *A Campaign From Santa Fe to the Mississippi* . . . . Shreveport, 1865; reprint ed. by Martin H. Hall and Edwin A. Davis, Houston: Stagecoach Press, 1961.

Paris, Comte de, *History of the Civil War in America.* 4 vols. Philadelphia: Porter and Coates, 1875-1888.

Polignac, C. J., "Polignac's Mission," *Southern Historical Society Papers,* XXXII, 365-371.

Ragan, Cooper K., ed., "The Diary of Captain George W. O'Brien, 1863," *Southwestern Historical Quarterly,* LXVII, 28-54, 235-246, 413-433.

Sawyer, William E. and Neal A. Baker, Jr., eds., "A Texan in the Civil War," *Texas Military History,* II, 275-278.

Smith, Rebecca, and Marion Mullins, eds., "The Diary of H. C. Medford, Confederate Soldier, 1864," *Southwestern Historical Quarterly,* XXXIV, 203-230.

Taylor, Richard, *Destruction and Reconstruction: Personal Experiences of the Late War.* New York, 1879; reprint ed. by Richard B. Harwell, New York: Longmans, Green and Co., 1955.

Tilley, Nannie M., ed., *Federals on the Frontier: The Diary of Benjamin F. McIntyre, 1862-1864.* Austin: University of Texas Press, 1963.

United States Navy Department, *Official Records of the Union and Confederate Navies in the War of the Rebellion.* 31 vols. Washington: Government Printing Office, 1894-1927.

United States War Department, *War of the Rebellion: A Compilation of the Official Records of the Union and Confederate Armies.* 70 vols. in 128. Washington: Government Printing Office, 1880-1901.

Walker, Charles W., "Battle of Prairie Grove," *Publications of the Arkansas Historical Association,* II, 354-361.

Winkler, Ernest W., ed., *Journal of the Secession Convention of Texas, 1861.* Austin: Austin Printing Co., 1912.

Woods, J. T., *Services of the Ninety-Sixth Ohio Volunteers.* Toledo: Blade Printing and Paper Co., 1874.

Wright, Mrs. D. Giraud, *A Southern Girl in '61; The War-Time Memories of a Confederate Senator's Daughter.* New York: Doubleday, Page and Company, 1905.

Yeary, Mamie, *Reminiscences of the Boys in Gray, 1861-1865.* Dallas: Smith and Lamar, 1912.

## II. Secondary Sources

Bentley, H. L., and Thomas Pilgrim, *The Texas Legal Directory for 1876-77*. Austin: Democratic Statesman Office, 1877.

*Biographical Encyclopedia of Texas*. New York: Southern Publishing Company, 1880.

*Biographical Souvenir of the State of Texas* . . . . Chicago: F. A. Battey and Company, 1889.

Brown, John Henry, *History of Dallas County, Texas, From 1837 to 1887*. Dallas: Milligan, Cornett and Farnham printers, 1887.

Cochran, John H., *Dallas County: A Record of Its Pioneers and Progress* . . . . Dallas: A. S. Mathis, Service Publishing Co., 1928.

Daniell, L. E., comp., *Personnel of the Texas State Government, with Sketches of Distinguished Texans* . . . . Austin: City Printing Company, 1887.

——————, *Personnel of the Texas State Government, with Sketches of Representative Men of Texas*. San Antonio: Maverick Printing House, 1892.

——————, *Types of Successful Men of Texas*. Austin: E. Von Boeckmann printer, 1890.

DeRyee, William, and R. E. Moore, comps., *The Texas Album of the Eighth Legislature, 1860*. Austin: Miner, Lambert and Perry, 1860.

Duncan, Merle Mears, "David Richard Wallace, Pioneer in Psychiatry," *Texana*, I, 341-362.

Ewing, Floyd F., Jr., "Origins of Unionist Sentiment on the West Texas Frontier," *West Texas Historical Association Year Book*, XXXII, 21-29.

——————, "Unionist Sentiment on the Northwest Texas Frontier," *West Texas Historical Association Year Book*, XXXIII, 58-70.

Hatton, Roy O., "Prince Camille de Polignac and the American Civil War, 1863-1865," *Louisiana Studies*, III, 163-195.

Heitman, Francis B., *Historical Register and Dictionary of the United States Army, from its Organization, September 29, 1789 to March 2, 1903*. 2 vols. Washington: Government Printing Office, 1903.

Irwin, Richard B., *History of the Nineteenth Army Corps*. New York: G. P. Putnam's Sons, 1892.

Johnson, Ludwell H., *Red River Campaign: Politics and Cotton in the Civil War*. Baltimore: Johns Hopkins University Press, 1958.

Landrum, Graham, *Grayson County, An Illustrated History of Grayson County, Texas*. Fort Worth: University Supply and Equipment Company, 1960.

Lemley, Harry J., "General de Polignac," *United Daughters of the Confederacy Magazine*, XXV, No. 10, p. 16.

Lonn, Ella, *Foreigners in the Confederacy*. Chapel Hill: University of North Carolina Press, 1940.

Lusk, R. M., *Constantine Lodge No. 13 Ancient, Free and Accepted Masons*. Bonham: Favorite Printing Co., 1917.

"Major General Prince Camille de Polignac, C. S. A.," *United Daughters of the Confederacy Magazine*, XX, No. 1, pp. 14-15, 19, 22.

*Members of the Legislature of the State of Texas from 1846 to 1939*. Austin, 1939.

*Memorial and Biographical History of Dallas County, Texas*. Chicago: The Lewis Publishing Company, 1892.

Oates, Stephen B., *Confederate Cavalry West of the River*. Austin: University of Texas Press, 1961.

Parks, Joseph H., *General Edmund Kirby Smith, C. S. A.* Baton Rouge: Louisiana State University Press, 1954.

Pierredon, Count Michel de, "Major General C. J. Polignac, C. S. A.," *Confederate Veteran*, XXII, 389.

Plummer, Alonzo H., *Battle of Mansfield or Sabine Cross Roads*. [Mansfield, 1963.]

Ragan, Cooper K., *Josephus Somerville Irvine, 1819-1876, The Worthy Citizen*. Houston, 1963.

Red, George Plunkett, *The Medicine Man in Texas*. Houston: Standard Printing and Lithographing Co., 1930.

Sawyer, William E., "Martin Hart, Civil War Guerrilla," *Texas Military History*, III, 146-153.

Sleeper, William M., and Allan D. Sanford, *Waco Bar and Incidents of Waco History*. Waco: Hill Printing and Stationery Company, 1947.

Smyrl, Frank H., Unionism, Abolitionism, and Vigilantism in Texas, 1856-1865. Master's thesis, University of Texas, 1961.

Stambaugh, J. Lee, and Lillian J. Stambaugh, *A History of Collin County, Texas*. Austin: Texas State Historical Association, 1958.

Warner, Ezra J., *Generals in Gray: Lives of the Confederate Commanders*. Baton Rouge: Louisiana State University Press, 1959.

Wheeler, L. T., "Gen. Wilbur[n] Hill King," *Confederate Veteran*, XIX, 172-173.

Winters, John D., *The Civil War in Louisiana*. Baton Rouge: Louisiana State University Press, 1963.

Wooster, Ralph A., "Analysis of the Membership of the Texas Secession Convention," *Southwestern Historical Quarterly,* LXII, 322-335.

Wooten, Dudley G., ed., *Comprehensive History of Texas, 1685-1897*. 2 vols. Dallas: William G. Scarff, 1898. Included are short sketches of the 31st and the 34th Texas, and the 11th Texas Battalion.

# INDEX

Alexander, Almerine M., 8; biographical sketch of, 2; commands brigade, 17-18; resigns, 19
Alexandria, Louisiana, 18, 19, 24, 28, 38, 42, 43, 44, 48
Alligator Lake, 47
Anderson, Texas, 54
Arkansas, 1, 4, 6, 8-12, 49-51
Arkansas Post, Arkansas, 21
Arkansas River, 11, 13, 15
Arms, 5, 6, 19, 21, 22, 23, 30, 31
Atchafalaya River, 20, 21, 22, 23, 24, 25, 27, 32, 33, 46, 47
Austin, Arkansas, 12

Bagby, A. P.: cavalry brigade of, 30, 44
Banks, Nathaniel P., 18, 20, 38, 39, 41, 44
Bass, Thomas Coke: biographical sketch of, 8; commands brigade, 8-9
Bastrop, Louisiana, 49
Bates, Joseph, 20
Baton Rouge, Louisiana, 25
Baylor, George W., 54
Bayou Bartholomew, 49
Bayou Bodcau, 51
Bayou Boeuf, 24, 28, 30, 44
Bayou Bourbeau: battle of, 30-32, poem about, 58-59
Bayou de Glaize, 33, 44, 45, 46
Bayou Fordoche, 33; battle of, see Stirling's Plantation, battle of
Bayou Lafourche, 20
Bayou Lamourie, 44
Bayou Rapides, 43
Bayou Rouge, 45
Bayou Teche, 18, 22, 27
Beasley's, Louisiana, 38
Beaumont, Texas, 23
Beaver Creek, 48
Bee, H. P., 55, 56
Belle Cheney Springs, Louisiana, 28
Bentonville, Arkansas, 6
Berwick Bay, Louisiana, 32
Bexar County, Texas, 5
Big Spring, Missouri, 7
Black River, 48
Blunt, James G., 10
Boeuf River, 49
Boggy Creek, 17
Bonham, Texas, 1, 2
Boone, H. H., 26
Border, John P.: regiment of, 54
Bowie County, Texas, 6
Bradfute, William R.: biographical sketch of, 9; commands brigade, 9-11
Bragg, Braxton, 48

Brashear City, Louisiana, 20, 21, 23
Brownsville, Texas, 56
Buck, John A., 48
Burbridge, S. G.: infantry brigade of, 30, 32
Bush, William M.: biographical sketch of, 2; wounded, 46

Camden, Arkansas, 50, 51
Camp Bayou Meto, Arkansas, 13
Camp Boggs, Louisiana, 48
Camp Bounty, Texas, 6
Camp Bragg, Arkansas, 50
Camp Coffee, Missouri, 7, 8
Camp Crocket, Texas, 12
Camp Daniel, Texas, 12
Camp Diarrhea, Louisiana, 22
Camp Kiamichi, Indian Territory, 17
Camp Nelson, Arkansas, 12
Camp Osage, Arkansas, 6
Camp Rogers, Texas, 55
Canadian River: North Fork of, 2
Cane River, 38, 42; engagement at mouth of, 43
Carencro Bayou, 24, 28
Carroll Jones's, Louisiana, 38
Carthage, Missouri, 6
Casualties, 7, 8, 11, 27, 32, 37, 38, 41, 43, 46
Caudle, John H., 43, 45, 46; promoted, 28
Centerville, Texas, 54
Central Texas, 2, 11
Champion No. 3, 42n
Champion No. 5, 42n
Cheneyville, Louisiana, 28, 30, 38, 44
Chicot, Louisiana, 28
Churchill, Thomas J.: infantry division of, 40, 41, 50
Clack, F. H.: infantry battalion of, 25
Clarksville, Arkansas, 11, 13
Clarksville, Texas, 5, 17, 19
Clear Bayou, 46
Cloutierville, Louisiana, 42
Coco's Plantation, Louisiana, 46
Coke, Richard: biographical sketch of, 12; wounded, 32
Collin County, Texas, 1, 2
Columbia, Louisiana, 35, 49
Concordia Lake, 36
Cooke County, Texas, 2
Cooper, Douglas H., 1, 2; biographical sketch of, 6; commands brigade, 6-8
Cornay, Florian O.: battery of, 43
Corsicana, Texas, 11, 12
Craven, Jesse L.: commands brigade, 9
Cricket, 42n

Kansas, 2
Kiamichi River, 15
King, Wilburn Hill, 30, 55; biographical sketch of, 50; commands brigade, 42, 50-53, promoted, 42
Kock's Plantation, Louisiana: engagement at, 20

Lafayette County, Arkansas, 51
Lake Louis, 49
Lecompte, Louisiana, 34, 38, 43, 44, 48
Likens, James B.: regiment of, 54
Little River, 37
Little Rock, Arkansas, 5, 6, 11, 12, 13, 50
Lloyd's bridge, Louisiana, 44
Logansport, Louisiana, 54
Losses, see Casualties
Louisiana, 18-49, 51-54, 55
Louisiana infantry brigade, see Mouton and Gray
Lyon's Ferry, Louisiana, 25

McCulloch, Henry E., 5, 6; infantry division of, 11, 13
McNutt's Hill, Louisiana, 43, 48
Madisonville, Texas, 54
Magruder, John B., 49, 50, 51, 55
Major, James P.: cavalry brigade of, 25, 30; cavalry division of, 39, 40, 44
Malone, Frederick J., 25; biographical sketch of, 5
Mansfield, Louisiana, 38; battle of, see Sabine Crossroads, battle of
Mansura, Louisiana, 33, 47; skirmish at, 44-45
Marksville, Louisiana, 19, 44, 47
Marmaduke, John S.: cavalry division of, 9
Maxey, Sam B., 54, 55, 56
Merrick, George W., 47; promoted, 48
Millican, Texas, 11, 12
Minden, Louisiana, 51, 52, 53
Mississippi River, 13, 20, 23, 32, 35; Confederate attempt to cross, 48
Missouri, 4, 6-8
Monett's Ferry, Louisiana, 42, 43
Monroe, Louisiana, 35, 49
Montgomery, Louisiana: engagement near, 42-43
Monticello, Arkansas, 49
Morale problems, 4, 9, 11, 13, 15-19, 23, 28, 29, 30, 33, 48, 49, 52, 55, 56
Moreauville, Louisiana, 46
Morgan's Ferry, Louisiana, 20, 24, 25, 27
Morganza, Louisiana, 23, 33
Moundville, Louisiana, 27, 28
Mount Enterprise, Texas, 54
Mount Pleasant, Texas, 19

Mouton, Alfred, 20, 27, 39; infantry brigade of, 20, 21, 25, 28, 33, 38; infantry division of, 38, 39
Muddy Boggy Creek, 17

Natchez, Mississippi, 35, 36
Natchitoches, Louisiana, 22, 38, 41, 42, 53, 55
Navasota, Texas, 56
Navy, Union, 36, 37, 38, 42, 43, 44, 47
Negro troops, Union, 35
New Iberia, Louisiana, 20, 22, 32
New Orleans, Louisiana, 20
Newtonia, Missouri: battle of, 7-8
Nineteenth Army Corps, 31
Noble, Sebron M., 21; killed, 39
North Texas, 1-5, 14
Norwood's Plantation, Louisiana: battle of, see Yellow Bayou, battle of
Notley, W. J., 52

Oldham, M. W.: poem by, 58-59
Opelousas, Louisiana, 20, 24, 29, 31
Ouachita River, 35, 36, 37, 49

Palestine, Texas, 54
Palo Pinto County, Texas, 2
Paris, Texas, 1, 5
Park Hill, Indian Territory, 6
Parsons, Mosby M.: infantry division of, 40, 41, 50
Pay, 5-6, 9, 12
Pea Ridge, Arkansas: battle of, mentioned, 4
Peak, William W.: company of, 5
Pike, Albert, 4
Pine Bluff, Arkansas, 49
Pineville, Louisiana, 38, 48
Pineville, Missouri, 8
Piney Bayou, 13, 14
Pleasant Hill, Louisiana, 38, 39, 54; battle of, 40-41
Polignac, Camille Armand Jules Marie, Prince de, 29, 33, 35-42, 45, 47, 50, 52; biographical sketch of, 21-22; commands brigade, 29-39; infantry division of, 39-53; promoted, 41; returns to France, 54
Polignac's Brigade: arms, 5, 19, 21, 22, 23, 30, 31; battles: Shirley's Ford, 6-7, Newtonia, 7-8, Prairie Grove, 10-11, Kock's Plantation, 20, Stirling's Plantation, 24-27, Bayou Bourbeau, 30-32, Vidalia, 36-37, Harrisonburg, 37-38, Sabine Crossroads, 39-40, Pleasant Hill, 40-41, Montgomery, 42-43, Cane River, 43, Yellow Bayou, 45-47; casualties, 7, 8, 11, 27, 32, 37, 38, 41, 43, 46; commanders: Cooper, 6-8, Bass, 8-9, Craven, 9, Bradfute, 9-11, Speight, 13-24, 28-29, Alexander, 17-18,

71

Travis County, Texas, 5
Trenton, Louisiana, 35
Trinity, Louisiana, 35, 37, 38, 48
Tucker, Thomas F., 52
Twentieth Texas Cavalry, 8-11, 13-15; dismounted, 9
Twentieth Texas Infantry, 55
Twenty-eighth Texas Cavalry, 55
Twenty-second Texas Cavalry, 1, 3, 4, 6-11, 13-19, 21, 28-30, 32, 33, 35-56; dismounted, 9; organized, 1-2
Tyler, Texas, 5

Unionist sentiment, 2, 3, 4, 9, 14, 15

Van Buren, Arkansas, 9, 13
Velasco, Texas, 11
Vermilion Bridge, Louisiana, 28
Vermilionville, Louisiana, 22, 23, 27
Vicksburg, Mississippi, 13, 20
Vidalia, Louisiana, 35; engagement at, 36-37
Ville Platte, Louisiana, 27

Waco, Texas, 11, 17
Walker, John G., 50; infantry division of, 19, 28, 30, 38, 39, 40, 41, 48, 49
Wallace, David R.: biographical sketch of, 11; letter of, 49
Waller's cavalry battalion, 25, 26
Walnut Hill, Arkansas, 51
Warren, Arkansas, 50
Washington, Arkansas, 12, 50
Washington, Louisiana, 20, 24, 27, 30
Weapons, see Arms
Weitzel's infantry division, 31
Wells' Texas Cavalry, 55
West, H. C.: battery of, 18
Western Louisiana, District of, 18
Wharton, John A., 43, 45, 46, 47, 50, 53, 54
Winnfield, Louisiana, 35
Wooten, George H., 2

Yellow Bayou: battle of 45-47